Walter S. McDowell

Broadcast Television

A Complete Guide to the Industry

PETER LANG
New York • Washington, D.C./Baltimore • Bern
Frankfurt am Main • Berlin • Brussels • Vienna • Oxford

Library of Congress Cataloging-in-Publication Data
McDowell, Walter S.
Broadcast television: a complete guide to the industry / Walter S. McDowell.
p. cm. — (Media industries; vol. 1)
Includes bibliographical references and index.
1. Television broadcasting—United States. I. Title.
PN1992.3.U5M29   384.550973—dc22   2006019922
ISBN 0-8204-8836-4 (hardcover)
ISBN 0-8204-7485-1 (paperback)
ISSN 1550-1043

Bibliographic information published by **Die Deutsche Bibliothek**.
Die Deutsche Bibliothek lists this publication in the "Deutsche
Nationalbibliografie"; detailed bibliographic data is available
on the Internet at http://dnb.ddb.de/.

Cover design by Lisa Barfield

The paper in this book meets the guidelines for permanence and durability
of the Committee on Production Guidelines for Book Longevity
of the Council of Library Resources.

∞

© 2006 Peter Lang Publishing, Inc., New York
29 Broadway, New York, NY 10006
www.peterlang.com

Printed in the United States of America

Broadcast Television

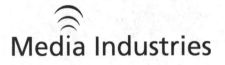

Media Industries

David Sumner
General Editor

Vol. 1

PETER LANG
New York • Washington, D.C./Baltimore • Bern
Frankfurt am Main • Berlin • Brussels • Vienna • Oxford

Contents

Preface

Why this book is different

Compared to most books dealing with television, this volume is somewhat unconventional for several reasons. First, it is concise, intended for a reader who wants to grasp the essentials of the television industry without being forced to endure volumes of irrelevant detail. Second, this book does not venture into the thicket of cultural criticism, assessing what is right or wrong with television. Recognizing that bookstores and libraries are already brimming with such commentaries and tirades, the purpose of this book is not to prove a point but rather to provide information the reader can use to make his or her own interpretations and judgments. To that end, this book attempts to take an impartial look at the inner workings of the *business* of commercial television and how economics, technology, and regulation influence business decisions. Third, unlike most textbooks that address a broad array of mass media from newspapers and magazines to satellites and the Internet, this book maintains a tighter focus by concentrating on conventional over-the-air television. This narrowed approach contributes not only to the brevity of the book but, more important, to the depth of knowledge provided.

Other media and new technologies are not ignored but are analyzed from the standpoint of their relationship with television.

In attempting to publish a book about such a dynamic topic as television, an unfortunate fact of life is the speed of change. Long after this book has gone to press, the technological, regulatory, and economic components of the television business will continue to evolve. Consequently, rather than providing a mere accumulation of soon-to-be obsolete facts, it is hoped that this book provides some enduring insights into what makes the television industry operate the way it does. As a result, the organization and presentation style of this work embraces the notion that the television industry is more than the sum of its parts and is indeed a web of relationships operating within a complex *system*.

Where to Begin?

Understanding the
Television Industry
as a System

In order to explain how a complex object "works," well-intentioned people often begin by dismantling the object into the tiniest of pieces, like a child taking apart an old wind-up clock, spreading the little wheels, springs, brackets, and screws on the floor, all in an attempt to understand the mechanism. The problem is that this deconstruction still cannot explain how the clock goes tick, tick, tick. A more enlightened approach examines not only the individual parts but also how the parts fit together and influence each other.

In a similar fashion, the goal of this book is to provide not only factual information about the various parts of the television industry but also an appreciation of the *relationships*—the interdependence—of these parts. Indeed, professionals working in the industry don't experience it as a conglomeration of isolated parts but rather as a very complex, interactive system. In other words, this book explains what makes the television industry *tick*. The recognition that the whole of any complex system is more than the mere sum of its parts is the foundation of a paradigm called general systems theory first described by Ludwig von Bertalanffy[1] in the 1960s. Although beginning as a biological concept, this approach has been applied to all kinds of circumstances, from electrical circuitry and computer software to social and business organizations such as television stations.[2] Today many business scholars maintain that companies, products, and technologies are "like a species in a biological ecosystem, increasingly intertwined in mutually dependent relationships."[3] System theory has been called the science of complexity.

Interdependence is the most important defining characteristic of this approach in that a system is the outcome of the interactions among its essential parts. In a complex system, such as an industry, many variables interrelate with one another, ultimately producing a kind of mosaic. Along these lines, this book attempts to examine many television industry variables while at the same time placing these components within a larger context of how the industry "works." Perhaps the term "variable" sounds too clinical and detached from the real world of television. After all, the true industry consists of flesh-and-blood people making decisions. Let us humanize the important factors involved with the television industry by identifying them not as variables but as players—players such as station and network executives, producers, directors, actors, news anchors, government officials, researchers, judges, and the most vital of industry players, audiences. From a systems approach, we recognize the interdependence of all these players within a highly competitive and ever-changing business environment.

Strategic Decision-Making

Players within a system must make decisions. A formal definition of strategic decision-making is *the allocation of scarce resources by individuals or groups to achieve goals under conditions of uncertainty and risk.*[4] For television stations and networks, the allocation of scarce resources typically includes decisions about investing in people, programming, marketing, research, and technology. The conditions of uncertainty involve predicting audience and advertiser demand and also predicting strategic maneuvers by competitors. The risk factor typically is the possible loss of audiences and subsequent loss of advertising revenue. It is hoped that this book will enable the reader to appreciate to some degree the circumstances in which decisions are made.

The Business of Television

Readers will realize early on that the term "industry" found in the title of this book refers to the business of television or, more precisely, commercial television. Social and cultural aspects cannot be ignored completely, but the essence of this book is an objective explanation of the business system that has stimulated so much discussion and debate over the past fifty years. Even a reader interested primarily in broadcast journalism should have some exposure to the business side of television because, as Les Moonves, chairman of CBS, once declared, "News is commerce too."[5] Of course, noncommercial or public television operates alongside the commercial networks and stations, and much has been written about its place within the larger system of American broadcasting. Although the study of noncommercial media is certainly a worthwhile pursuit, it is not the highly focused topic of this book.

Commercial television in this country makes use of a two-phase business model in which stations and networks develop business strategies that address two distinct target groups, namely audiences and advertisers. While audience-based business strategies are aimed primarily at the general public, advertiser-based business strategies concentrate on a much smaller audience of business decision-makers, people who actually buy what television is selling, namely audiences. Of course, no advertiser would purchase commercial time on a station or network that no one is watching!

What Do We Mean by the Term *Television?*

For decades, television was easy to define, but in recent years the very definition of the term has been questioned. For example, in 2005 the revered weekly trade publication *Broadcasting and Cable*, read by most of the above-mentioned industry players, added the slogan "The business of television" to its redesigned masthead. Obviously, the editors now perceive the once-unique industries of conventional television broadcasting and cable as essentially the same thing—television. Indeed, other publications aimed at both business professionals and the general public have begun to merge editorially the two industries when talking about topics such as "networks," "commercials," and "ratings." This trend makes sense in many respects, because today most viewers, when using a remote control or computer mouse, cannot distinguish a cable channel from a broadcast channel. The buzz phrase technological convergence, fostered by the adoption of digital communication, has blurred the once-familiar distinctions among not only broadcast television and cable but all kinds of mediated communication. Conventional print and electronic media content can now be digitized and offered to consumers through a variety of electronic sources or "platforms," including over-the-air broadcast, satellite, microwave, cable, telephone, fiber optics, and the

Internet. Essentially, content is no longer unalterably attached to any particular delivery device.

Digital technology has also influenced the manner in which we consume media. Our everyday vocabulary has been transformed by phrases such as *time-shifting*, *multi-tasking*, *zapping*, and *wireless access*, all of which influence where, when, and how we consume "television."

Coinciding with the convergence of media technologies has been the convergence of media businesses, commonly referred to as consolidation. Beginning with the groundbreaking 1996 Telecommunications Act, there has been an ongoing agenda to dismantle cross-ownership restrictions among television stations, radio stations, cable systems, and newspapers. As digital convergence continues to break down technological barriers, so media companies want to break down what they believe to be obsolete ownership barriers that forbid the development of exciting business synergies. These new relationships are fostering systems within systems.

So what do we mean by the television industry today? To take an overly wide view in which any type of video would be considered television would be overwhelming for the reader and beyond the scope of a short book. Despite the fact that many audiences cannot describe differences among broadcast, cable, and satellite program content, the technological, regulatory, and economic business components underlying these industries are quite different and deserve special attention. In this vein, Peter Lang Publishing for this series decided to address each with a separate book. Of course, there is an obvious overlap among these media, but for the sake of clarity and conciseness, we will define the television industry according to its traditional boundaries of *over-the-air television stations and their networks*. This will be our nexus or hub for all discussion. Of course, networks and stations are becoming increasingly involved in all sorts of cross-media ventures, particularly with cable and the Internet. These burgeoning business opportunities will be addressed, but always from the vantage point of the television broadcaster.

Adding a Dash of History

Most systems have a history, and as a result this book presents—where appropriate—a dash of television history. Understanding how and why a system works today often requires a brief look backward. The design and substance of today's television industry did not pop up suddenly out of nowhere. Instead, it has deep technological, regulatory, and economic roots in the history of this country. What is past becomes prelude to our future. Additionally, two case-study chapters are included to describe how the system adapts and changes over time.

The Challenge of Explanation

If a system is, indeed, more than the sum of its parts, how does an author organize a book about television as a business system? The real dilemma is that before we can understand the relationship among the parts of a system, we first need to understand each part. Consequently, this book is divided into distinct chapters or parts, but one will experience a concerted effort to integrate each chapter topic into a larger whole, in the hope that the reader will gain an appreciation of both the parts and the process.

Recognizing the inevitable overlap in creating categories for presentation, the remainder of this book has been divided into nine chapters. Chapter 2 begins the journey with a brief overview of the technology of television, emphasizing the implications stemming from the industry's eagerly awaited transition from analog to digital transmission. Chapters 3 and 4 look at the television business model and how television broadcasters attempt to attract audiences and then sell these audiences to advertisers. Chapter 5 takes a law-and-policy perspective, explaining some of the challenges of regulating television in a culture of free enterprise. Chapter 6 introduces the reader to the all-important but highly controversial world of audience research and ratings. Chapter 7 is a case study that helps explain how the industry can function, fail, adapt, and evolve over time. Chapter 8 reveals how the sometimes rocky relationship between stations and networks may serve as a bellwether for the future of the television industry. Chapter 9 synthesizes the information presented in earlier chapters and speculates about what is on the horizon for the American system of television.

Returning to our wind-up-clock analogy for understanding the relationships of parts as well as the parts themselves, perhaps this is no longer a perfect metaphor, because today almost all clocks are solid-state electronic devices with few if any moving parts. This does not mean that relationships do not exist, just that the clock configurations are electronic rather than mechanical. In the 1960s, media scholar and philosopher Marshall McLuhan spoke of an electronically configured world few could comprehend at the time. But today, much of what he said seems remarkably prophetic.

> Our electronically configured world has forced us to move from the habit of data classification to the mode of pattern recognition. We can no longer build serially, block by block, step by step, because instant communication insures that all factors of the environment and of experience coexist in a state of active interplay.[6]

The author hopes that a reader of this brief book will acquire not only an accumulation of worthwhile facts about the television industry but also an appreciation of the "active interplay" of those facts.

Questions for Further Thought

1   Apply a *systems approach* to a personal job experience. Describe your duties in terms of how you *interacted* with other people or other departments and how your combined efforts contributed to the overall purpose of the business.

2   A formal definition of strategic decision-making is *the allocation of scarce resources by individuals or groups to achieve goals under conditions of uncertainty and risk.* Based on your personal job experience, describe

   a   The resources that had to be allocated, such as money, time, materials, and labor.

   b   The conditions of uncertainty, such as lack of knowledge about customers and competitors.

   c   The risk factors involved, such as the possible loss of money, employees, or reputation.

3   Provide an example of *media convergence* in your personal life in which you move content around from one medium to another, such as downloading video.

Sending Pictures through the Air

Understanding Television's Technology

Regardless of all the interrelated components of the television industry, there must be a beginning in technology. Without the science of television, the business of television would not exist. And so we begin this book with a brief explanation of how analog television works and how the transition to digital television will soon dramatically alter the way audiences and advertisers experience television. Although we focus on technical matters in this chapter, the influence of government regulation will become obvious. Government agencies, most notably the Federal Communications Commission (FCC), have attempted to respond to the needs of new technology, and new technology, in turn, has evolved in accordance with the mandates of government. These interactions have occurred within the economic context of television being a profit-driven business venture. Understanding some of the fundamental physics of broadcasting allows a student of media to better understand the origins of government regulation and the development of the broadcast business model.

In the Beginning

As with the introduction of other radically new technologies, many "experts" in the 1930s refused to see the promise of television and quickly discounted its future importance. A 1939 editorial in the *New York Times* predicted that in coming years television would be no more than a novelty.

> The problem with television is that people must sit and keep their eyes glued to the screen; the average American family hasn't time for it. Therefore, the showmen are convinced that for this reason, if for no other, television will never be a serious competitor of broadcasting.[1]

Others embraced television with a misplaced optimism, believing that the technology would bring everlasting peace to the planet. In 1946, a syndicated newspaper column entitled Here Is Television: Your Window on the World boasted that "television should do more to develop friendly neighbors, and to bring understanding and peace on earth, than any single material force in the world today."

Obviously, neither prediction was accurate, as predicting the impact of new technology on human behavior has always been more conjecture than science. But after decades of relatively few dramatic technological changes, American television is on the brink of a revolution. We begin with an explanation of how conventional analog television works.

Analog Television

If you restored an "antique" television set, one manufactured in the 1950s, and attached a simple antenna, you could still receive recognizable pictures and sound from a modern television station. Of course the picture would be in black and white, and the sound would not be in stereo, but it would nonetheless still be what engineers call *analog television*. For decades, the basic analog television standard has served the United States well. Improvements have been made periodically, but the core operating principles have remained unchanged.

Conventional analog television begins with a video camera taking a picture of a scene at a frame rate of thirty frames per second, similar to a motion picture camera capturing images frame by frame on a film negative. A major difference is that a television camera processes these images electronically, rather than chemically, into rows of individual dots called pixels. Each pixel is assigned a color and intensity. The lines of pixels are combined with synchronization signals called *horizontal sync* and *vertical sync*, enabling the electronics of a receiving television set to interpret properly the original scene into a *composite video signal*. Sound is completely separate from the visual portion of the scene and is acquired and recorded in the same manner as FM radio. The clarity of a television picture is called its *resolution*. An analog television set can display 525 horizontal lines of resolution every thirtieth of a second. In reality, however, an analog television displays half of those lines in one-sixtieth of a second, and then displays the other half in the next sixtieth, so the whole frame is updated every one-thirtieth of a second. This process is called interlacing. This process, plus fewer scan lines and pixel shape, makes resolution so disappointing when compared to computer-based digital processing.[2]

A television station uses a transmitting tower with an antenna to distribute or *radiate* its video and audio signals in a roughly circular pattern to home receivers located within approximately a sixty-mile radius of the station's tower. Because of the unique propagation characteristics of television and FM radio waves, a television station's signal is restricted to *line-of-sight*, or the horizon. Therefore, the height of the tower, as well as the electrical power assigned by the FCC to a transmitter, essentially determines how far a television signal can travel. These geographical limitations fostered the creation of interconnected station networks.

When a composite video signal is broadcast by a television station, it happens on a specific frequency or *channel*. In the United States, these are identified as *Very High Frequency (VHF)* channels 2 through 13 and *Ultra High Frequency (UHF)* channels 14 through 83. Although numerically the channel numbers appear to be contiguous along the same spectrum line, in reality they are separated into two distinct channel groupings separated by the services, such as the entire FM radio band and aviation, positioned between channels 6 and 7. As a result, the frequencies assigned to channels 7 and above are considerably higher than what the simple channel numbers depict. As will be revealed later in this chapter, this seemingly inconsequential arrangement of channels has been the source of much anguish and frustration among UHF broadcasters.[3]

The introduction of radio in the 1920s found that signal interference between two or more stations operating on the same or nearly the same frequency resulted in an unacceptable weakening and distortion of all signals. In 1927 a government official described the chaos caused by interference:

> . . . interference between broadcasters on the same wavelength became so bad at many points on the dial that the listener might suppose instead of a receiving set he had a peanut roaster with assorted whistles. Indeed every human ingenuity and selfish impulse seemed to have been exerted to complicate the tangle in the ether.[4]

Because there were only a finite number of frequencies available, and the use of adjacent frequencies fostered unwanted interference, the legal notion of *scarcity of spectrum* justified early government intervention in the development of broadcasting. The 1927 Radio Act and later the 1934 Communications Act established a regulatory framework that remains essentially intact today.[5] Unlike print media, where two competing newspapers or magazines could theoretically operate their presses next door to one another, the close proximity of radio and television signals presents all kinds of reception problems.

Because a television station's signal is indeed local, stations around the country can share the same channel designation without interference, as long as there is adequate geographical separation between transmitting towers. (A rule of thumb has been about two hundred miles.) In addition to assigning channels, the FCC stipulates maximum operating power, tower height, and sometimes directional restrictions on a station's transmission.[6]

These licensed stations are clustered into communities or *markets*. Today the United States sustains about 1,200 commercial stations located in 210 designated markets. Some markets are highly populated, such as New York, Los Angeles and Chicago, while others are tiny in comparison, such as Fargo, North Dakota; Monterey, California; and Gainesville, Florida. In addition to single-city markets, the system also includes many multiple-city or hyphenated markets, such as Albany-Schenectady-Troy, Orlando-Daytona Beach-Melbourne, and Dallas-Fort Worth. Most markets support between four and six commercial stations, along with one or two noncommercial operations. In theory, the geographical signal patterns or coverage contours of all stations within the same market are supposed to be approximately the same, but the industry has many exceptions, especially in hyphenated markets, in which the FCC-designated city of license and tower location for each station may be different. Before the *retransmission* of television signals by wired cable systems became common, a station's over-the-air geographical coverage area was often a crucial factor in determining the financial success or failure of a station, particularly among stations assigned to a UHF channel.

Full Power versus Low Power Stations

For over forty years, all television stations were considered "full power," but in 1984 the FCC introduced Low Power Television, or LPTV, as an added television service, issuing licenses and assigning channels in a manner almost identical to full power stations. The most obvious exception was that indeed these new stations had to operate using substantially less power, resulting in a signal coverage area of only ten or fifteen miles. At the time of its inception, the lofty goal of LPTV, according to the FCC, was to provide opportunities for locally oriented television programming "tailored to the interests of viewers in small localized areas, providing a means of local self-expression."[7] In fact, in recent years the official name of the service has been altered from LPTV to community television, and many station owners belong to the Community Broadcasters Association (CBA).[8] This low power service was created at a time when American commercial television was dominated by an oligopoly of three networks (ABC, CBS, and NBC) and noncommercial television (that is, public television) was not providing sufficient diversity in programming. Despite its high aspirations, this service has struggled to survive, and critics allege that new media technologies, such as digital cable, home satellite, and the Internet, have made these tiny over-the-air stations obsolete. As American television embarks on its historic transition to digital transmission, low power community television is at a critical juncture in its rocky history.

Networking

Networking, which began in the 1940s, is almost as old as television itself. Radio network giants CBS and NBC were quick to enter the television business. Later, ABC and the ill-fated DuMont network joined the network ranks. For the past decade, the system has consisted of six primary English-language networks—ABC, CBS, NBC, Fox, UPN, WB, and PAX. Only months before the writing of this book, PAX changed its name to "i" (as in "independent"), and rumors were flying that the small network was about to go under. In January 2006, the industry was startled to discover that UPN and WB were going to merge to form a new network, CW, reflecting the two corporate partners CBS, which owns UPN, and Warner Brothers. The obvious fallout from this merger will be that some stations (either UPN or WB affiliates) will become network orphans. At the writing of this book Fox had just created a small secondary network to accommodate some of these abandoned stations. Two Hispanic networks, Univision and Telemundo (owned by NBC), have made major strides in attracting Spanish-speaking audiences. Of course PPS is also a network but operates as a noncommercial entity.

For many years, network programming was supplied to affiliated stations via thousands of miles of *coaxial cable* rented to the networks by AT&T. As one might imagine, connecting hundreds of stations across the country was expensive, and the networks were eager to find a more efficient technology to achieve the same purpose. Satellite technology was the answer. By the late 1970s, most stations had the capability of receiving network and syndicated programming using a large, dish-shaped antenna called a *downlink*. Of course this highly cost-efficient technological breakthrough was not lost on the cable industry, which soon began to offer dozens and eventually hundreds of program networks to local cable outlets, which in turn distributed the programming via wire to individual cable subscribers. By the 1990s, satellite technology had become so sophisticated that *satellite-to-home* service, such as DirecTV, became a competitor of cable.[9] One point of confusion for many people has been the fact that satellite providers often refer to their program offerings as "cable networks," even though the satellite subscriber receiving this programming has no connection to a local cable company. Confounding this problem is the added semantic problem that both cable and satellite services offer programming from not only cable networks but also from the major broadcast networks (such as ABC, CBS, NBC, and so on). Although most audiences couldn't care less about the differences between a cable television network versus a *broadcast* television network (just another click on the remote), for the professionals who work in these industries, the differences are obvious and important.

In this age of pervasive subscription-based cable and satellite services, a student of media needs to remember that conventional television involves *over-the-air signals* radiating from a tall tower, and these signals are available to the public *free of charge*. Hence the phrase "free over-the-air broadcasting" has been used by defenders of the medium, such as the National Association of Broadcasters, when doing battle with the cable and satellite industries. One nagging controversy has been the ramifications of cable and satellite services retransmitting to subscribers "free" over-the-air broadcast programming. As will be discussed in more detail in later chapters, the technology of cable and satellite retransmission (that is, acquiring a television signal off air and distributing it to subscriber households) is relatively simple, but the intertwined legal and economic issues are quite complex.

The UHF Problem

Sometimes the development of an industry is influenced profoundly by a single event or a single decision. Such was the case in the television industry with the introduction of UHF channels. Looking back, few people predicted the devastating, long-term consequences of a decision made by the FCC way back in 1952. But first, let us set the stage.

During the war years (1941–45), commercial television lay dormant, but the stature of television would soon change dramatically. With the war restriction lifted, commercial license applications to the Federal Communications Commission (FCC) soared. In 1945, the FCC established a table of television channel assignments for the country. That same year the commission became increasingly aware that its station allocation plan was inadequate and decided that further expansion of television should cease until a better plan was designed. At the heart of the issue was *signal interference*. Only a small number of stations could operate in any one community, and this restriction was far worse for television than radio. While many large U.S. cities could accommodate a dozen or more radio stations, the number of television stations was usually limited to no more than three VHF stations. In order to satisfy the demand for licenses and cope with a limited supply of channels, the commission needed to go beyond VHF and become involved in the untried technology of the UHF spectrum. According to many scholars, faulty assumptions about the technology of television led to regulatory decisions that would devastate the UHF sector of American television for decades. Among the unintended consequences would be the dominance of the heavily VHF-based Big Three networks.[10]

In 1952, after a forty-three-month "freeze" on station licensing, the FCC finally decided on a new master allocation plan. The historic Sixth Report and Order of 1952 established over seventeen hundred commercial assignments within the United States, distributed to approximately twelve hundred communities. Of these, approximately five thousand were VHF and thirteen hundred UHF. One of the crucial underpinnings of the order was that it regarded UHF and VHF as technological equals that could therefore be intermixed within the same market.[11] Of course, in 1952, there was neither a single UHF transmitter nor a UHF home receiver in the entire country. Despite the misgivings of experts, most notably Alan B. DuMont, who was attempting to create a viable fourth network, the commission was convinced that even if there were some initial handicaps with this untried technology, "there is no reason to believe that American science will not produce the equipment necessary for the full development of UHF." Ignoring proposals for designating separate all-VHF and all-UHF markets, the commission refused to allow what it perceived as transitory technical problems with intermixture to obscure the long-range goal of a nationwide competitive television service.

In evaluating the quality of television signal reception, a simple gauge is that the higher the channel number, the lower the picture quality. Under the best of circumstances, watching UHF television in the 1950s was an ordeal, often filled with annoying static and noise.

Not all of the FCC commissioners agreed with the supposed wisdom of the Sixth Report and Order. Commissioner Robert F. Jones was the most vocal dissenter, maintaining that instead of solving a critical problem, the commission merely created "a bigger Frankenstein." Jones believed that the UHF-VHF intermixture policy "arbitrarily and adversely affected the ability of UHF stations to compete."[12] He was right. Over the next three decades, hundreds of UHF stations would fail.

In addition to rolling the dice on introducing and intermixing UHF transmission, a factor conspicuously missing from the FCC ruling was a mandate for all television set manufacturers to begin making home sets that were UHF compatible. Instead, the commission decided that market forces would address this potential problem without the need for government intervention. Imagine the insurmountable obstacle facing UHF broadcasters with hardly anyone in the country owning a television set that could actually receive a UHF signal. And, if someone did own a receiver with "all-channel capability," the UHF tuning control and antenna were far more difficult to operate compared to the same devices intended for VHF reception.

The UHF receiver problem continued to fester. Facing staggering debt and with no hope of sustaining a network comprised primarily of UHF affiliates, the DuMont network stopped operations in 1955, abandoning hundreds of stations with no alternative but to become *independent stations*. By 1961, the production of all-channel television sets (capable of receiving UHF as well as VHF channels) had fallen to a record low of 5.5 percent of all new sets. Independent UHF stations (with no network affiliation) were failing all over the country. The set manufacturers were reluctant to install voluntarily UHF hardware, because the installation added to the overall cost of producing a set, and there appeared to be little consumer demand for UHF service. On the other hand, frustrated broadcasters argued that, of course, there was no demand for programming originating from UHF stations because people lacked the necessary technology to even watch![13] Finally, in 1962, the All-Channel Receiver Bill became law, requiring set manufacturers to provide UHF equipment beginning in 1964—over a decade after the Sixth Report and Order was issued.[14] Even with universal UHF receiving requirements in place, it would be almost another decade before UHF-VHF dial-tuning standards (location, legibility, accuracy, and so on) would be enforced.

This chapter dwells on this particular technological issue because until recently it has had an enormous effect on the development of the television industry as a business. In terms of economic success, the television industry for decades was divided roughly into the VHF "haves" and the UHF "have nots." From the demise of the DuMont network in 1955, over thirty years would elapse before a viable fourth network using UHF stations could take hold and survive. One long-shot proposal made by Alan DuMont just before the Sixth Report and Order was made law was to revoke all VHF station licenses and start over with a fresh all-UHF service.[15]

Looking back, one can only guess how the industry would have evolved given a technologically level playing field for all broadcasters. The UHF calamity surfaces again in chapter 8, when we compare the demise of the DuMont network in the 1950s with the rise of the Fox network in the 1990s, a case study demonstrating the historic entanglements of technology, regulation, and economics.

One Technology Rescues Another

What rescued UHF television from its misery was yet another technology—cable. In an instant, as soon as a UHF station was included on a cable system's channel offerings, all the frustrating problems of poor over-the-air signal reception were eliminated by the miracle of "the wire." During the 1980s, as the number of cable subscriptions grew, so did the viewership of UHF stations. No doubt, cable could be seen as a rival to broadcasting, stealing away audiences to new cable networks, but it was also seen as a technological savior for these estranged broadcasters. Better signal reception meant better audience ratings, and better ratings inevitably meant better revenue.

The Dawn of Digital

Fifty years after the introduction of UHF, the television industry today faces several hauntingly familiar challenges. During the 1940s, four interrelated television industry issues surfaced almost simultaneously. First, the FCC conceded that the only means of satisfying the enormous demand for television station licenses was to make use of a promising but untried technology, namely UHF transmission. Second, with the introduction of UHF, the commission was then compelled to reallocate many station channel frequencies for the entire country. Third, corresponding with these actions, virtually all home television sets were made obsolete. To accommodate this new technology, set manufacturers were asked to modify voluntarily their internal components to allow for reception of UHF channels. Finally, in order to take advantage of the new technology, ordinary citizens had to discard their current television sets and buy new ones.

Fast-forwarding to the present day, we are experiencing similar circumstances. First, the FCC has mandated a monumental technological changeover from established analog transmission to untried digital transmission. Coinciding with this transformation is a total reallocation of the nation's channel frequencies. In addition, as the industry goes digital, television set manufacturers must eventually stop making analog television sets and provide new digital receivers. This means that every analog television set in the country will become obsolete, compelling ordinary citizens to discard their current television sets and buy new ones or purchase some type of set-top converter that will translate digital signals back to conventional analog displays.

American television today is embarking on a technological transition that rivals what occurred in the 1950s with the Sixth Report and Order. This metamorphosis from analog transmission to digital television (DTV) will cost billions of dollars, but the benefits will be many, including wide-screen, high-definition pictures (HDTV), viewer interaction, and simultaneous Internet access. From a program-networking perspective, DTV will also offer stations the option to circumvent one-channel HDTV in favor of broadcasting multi-channel standard-definition format (SDTV). Using these six or more additional channels, stations can join forces to form ad hoc digital networks that may or may not be associated with their old primary network. Of course, the cable industry is most reluctant to accept these added channels for retransmission on their systems without some kind of compensation. This issue will be elaborated in a later chapter.

In 1990, the FCC outlined a *simulcast* strategy whereby broadcasters will transmit both the new DTV signal and the existing analog signal concurrently for a period of time, at the end of which the analog channel would be discontinued and given back to the government. In 1998, the FCC put the final touches on its *Table of Allotments*, which includes digital channels 2 through 51.[16] The exact deadline for completion of this task by stations has been postponed several times, but by 2007 most stations will have slowly but surely made the conversion. The current deadline for permanently shutting down all analog transmissions is 2009. Because existing station production and transmission equipment must be replaced, this process is expensive and time consuming. Many stations operating in small markets have found this transition to be especially burdensome. Furthermore, until each individual market achieves a threshold of 85 percent digital television set penetration among households, stations must broadcast their original analog signal in parallel with their digital output. Judging by the rather modest retail purchase figures so far, this 85 percent threshold seems a long way away. Until the general public purchases digital television sets and the cable industry agrees to carry a station's digital sub-channels, the promise of DTV will not be realized completely.

Why Digital?

The main problem with analog television is resolution. The crispness, image stability, color, and detail in the picture cannot compare to the images generated from digital television. The drive toward digital has been fueled in part by the desire to give television the same resolution as a computer screen. For instance, the worst computer monitors you can buy have up to ten times more pixels than a conventional television set. (After spending considerable time watching a computer, the picture on a conventional television set seems fuzzy.) Unlike the 525 scanning lines used by analog television, an HDTV picture can have up to 1,080 lines, allowing for stunning picture detail. In brief, to improve picture resolution, digital television uses (a) more pixels, (b) smaller pixels, and (c) pixels that are closer together than analog television.[17]

In addition to better resolution, high-definition television can be used to display spectacular, wide-screen program content similar in format to a motion picture theater screen (that is, a 16:9 aspect ratio versus a 4:3 for ordinary television). Like the wide-screen movie formats, the HDTV screen is formatted much closer to the way humans see naturally in that our field of vision is more rectangular than square. So, when we view movies in wide-screen format, the image fills more of our field of vision and has a stronger visual impact. High-definition television programs can include Dolby digital surround sound, the same digital sound system used in movie theaters and on DVDs. Movies and sporting events, in particular, are well suited for high-definition television.

To date, the only digital television sets sold have been wide-screen devices, and these are quite expensive compared to conventional sets. However, the government has mandated that beginning in 2007, all television sets, including less expensive smaller units, must have DTV tuners installed. They will also have the new screen ratios to view HDTV. Nevertheless, Americans are still buying over twenty million analog sets each year, all of which will be rendered obsolete sometime in the near future.

Besides offering audiences wide-screen HDTV on one digital channel, station operators have the option to provide multiple *sub-channels*. Each sub-channel can carry a different program. The idea of sending multiple programs is unique to digital television and is made possible by a process called *digital compression*. Broadcasting multiple channels, or *multicasting*, has its technological trade-offs in that HDTV cannot be offered on all channels. A broadcaster can choose from a variety of resolutions depending on the type of program content being aired. For example, a televised sporting event, featuring many action scenes, probably would require more digital "bits" than a more static talk-show program. Soon, a typical day for a digital broadcaster might include multicasting three or four sub-channels during daytime hours and then switching to a single high-quality HDTV channel in prime time.

Receiving any type of DTV signal over the air requires an antenna and a new DTV receiver that can decode the digital signals. Cable and direct broadcast satellite (DBS) subscribers will also need a new DTV receiver and other special equipment to receive DTV programming. A "Plug-and-Play" or "Digital Cable Ready" DTV or other device for digital cable customers plugs directly into the cable jack and does not require a separate set-top box. As with most new consumer electronics technologies, DTV sets have become less expensive since their introduction. Prices are expected to continue to decrease over time and will vary depending on screen size, display technology, and other features. As of the writing of this book, only a tiny portion of American homes has purchased a digital receiver, and therefore the 85 percent penetration target appears to be many years away. Until the transition to DTV is complete, television stations will continue broadcasting on both their digital and analog channels.

Cable to the Rescue Again

Just as cable became the technological savior of UHF television, the cable industry and, to a lesser degree, the home satellite industry—with a combined 87 percent national household penetration—will play a vital role in getting digital television established throughout the country. Because to date so few households own a digital television set that can receive over-the-air signals, cable and satellite *retransmission* is the short-term technological solution for reaching audiences. Even after analog broadcasting stops completely, cable and satellite subscribers will be able to use their old analog television sets by attaching a special set-top converter. This device will receive DTV signals and change them into the format of the conventional television. For people not subscribing to cable or satellite, over-the-air broadcast converters will be available at retail stores. Of course, even with a converter, the analog television will not display the full picture quality of the DTV transmission. Around the country, stations have negotiated deals with local cable operators to carry some of their digital sub-channels.

One interesting proposal for accelerating the shutting down of analog transmissions has been to include in the overall calculations not only the purchase of digital television sets but also the use of cable- or satellite-provided set-top converters. Admittedly, these hybrid converter homes still cannot view pure, digitally enhanced programming, but the proposal in theory would allow stations to discontinue over-the-air analog transmissions much earlier. The government is supposed to use the retrieved analog spectrum for new uses.

Taking a broader systems approach to the digital transition, we see some economic issues that can't help but have an impact on the technological adoption of digital television and particularly HDTV. From an audience perspective, the restrictive cost of buying new digital sets must be addressed by the consumer marketplace. One factor often overlooked by analysts is that most households currently have more than one television set. A second issue pertains to the attractiveness of HDTV to broadcasters in that the enhanced quality of the picture does not translate directly to enhanced profits. That is, can broadcasters charge more for commercial time in HDTV programming, regardless of the size of the audience? So far, the advertising community is not doing cartwheels over the introduction of digital high definition. On the other hand, the notion of multicasting on digital sub-channels has gotten the attention of many local station operators who see opportunities to make money selling commercial time on new content outlets.

Technological Convergence

For decades, conventional media, such as newspapers, magazines, books, radio programs, television programs, movies, sound recordings, and telephone, were distinct technologies that fostered individual industries. However, with expanding digital technology, the partitions separating one medium from another are disappearing. This blurring of media boundaries or *media convergence* presents both perils and promises for over-the-air television broadcasters. Today, most media companies owning television stations or networks invest in other non-broadcast media platforms. For example, most television station news departments have established complementary Internet websites providing additional information on stories presented during a conventional newscast. Stations have been offering archived news story video on their websites for several years now.[18] With fewer viewers at home to watch daytime shows, a growing number of television stations are launching customized online newscasts. Usually abbreviated versions of over-the-air newscasts, the online shows offer two to five minutes' worth of headlines, weather, and traffic updates. Another new high-tech offering is cell phone alert systems to warn viewers when severe weather approaches. Some stations stream their complete half-hour or one-hour television newscasts in real time. Creating a long-form newscast designed specifically for the Internet is the latest in a wave of high-tech innovations, as local broadcasters search for new ways to deliver information to viewers on the go. Station executives say startup costs for these services are negligible, because for the most part they use existing news facilities and people.

In the wake of the digital revolution, many media companies both large and small are establishing partnerships with once-divergent media. For example, in Tampa, Florida, Media General has created much publicity since it merged the operations of the *Tampa Tribune* newspaper with television station WFLA-TV and an internet-based news service, *Tampa Bay Online*.[19] The catalyst energizing these partnerships is the effortlessness of using digital communication among different media "platforms." For instance, a news reporter, without leaving his or her desk, can provide text and video on a story that can be disseminated through (a) a scheduled television newscast, (b) a continuously "streamed" update for a news website, and (c) an in-depth summary article for the next day's newspaper.

The Impact of Emerging Video Technology

Emerging video technology, such as *video-on-demand* (VOD) channels and *digital video recorders* (DVRs), are cultivating a new media marketplace where audiences are no longer shackled by arbitrary program schedules imposed by broadcasters. Instead, through "time-shifting," viewers can acquire program content at any time. Similarly, *wireless access* to the Internet and other multi-channel services enable people to acquire program content at any location. People can download entire programs onto their cell phones or iPods, adding a new dimension of portability to television. The saving of television programming has evolved from film, to videotape, to digital computer files and servers.[20]

Obviously, the economic and regulatory fallout from digital communications is huge. Of particular interest is the burning question of how to make money. For example, the above-mentioned reincarnations of a television newscast into cable, Internet, and cell phone programming ventures have yet to generate much advertising revenue. The new technology is impressive, but the associated business models are still in development. Should these innovative services be subscription-based, or can the traditional thirty-second "spot announcement" still be of value in the digital age?

One example of how a digitally inspired device might have a profound effect on the television industry is the growing popularity of digital video recorders (DVRs) such as TiVo that permit audiences not only to time-shift programs but also to bypass or "zap" commercials. If these messages are no longer being seen by significant numbers of viewers, what is the value of commercial time for an advertiser? Despite the marvels of new technology, the system of American television broadcasting remains a business of attracting both audiences and advertisers.

 ## Questions for Further Thought

1 Based on your personal experience, what percentage of U.S. television set owners today do you think understand what digital television really is? What percentage of these people do you think realize that eventually their analog television sets will be obsolete?

2 Given the fact that 87 percent of all U.S. homes today subscribe to either cable or satellite, do you believe that some television stations should be allowed to simply turn off their antenna transmitters?

3 What arguments can you make that America's transition to digital transmission will or will not be similar to the struggle the industry experienced when attempting to introduce UHF television?

4 What do you envision as the role of cable in helping or hampering the expansion of digital television—both HDTV and multicasting?

5 Applying a systems approach to the transition to digital television, describe the web of relationships among consumers, television broadcasters, regulators (FCC), and even other media (such as cable) that will eventually make digital commonplace.

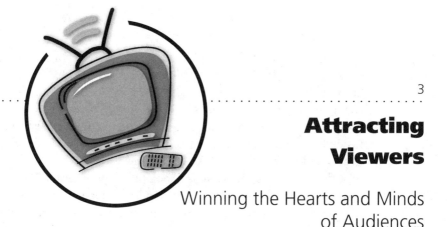

Attracting Viewers

Winning the Hearts and Minds of Audiences

Writer Paddy Chayefsky saw the irony of America's preoccupation with television when he said, "Television is the menace that everyone loves to hate but can't seem to live without."[1] Although the true business of broadcasting ultimately is the selling of audiences to advertisers, the first goal must be to attract audiences. Obviously people want to watch television. The challenge for television professionals is to persuade audiences to watch their station or network instead of the competition's. This is accomplished through the art and science of programming. In this respect, programming can be construed as the cost of doing business. Just as a car manufacturer must invest in materials and labor in order to produce a product for sale, so the television broadcaster must invest in programming in order to produce audiences for sale. No one needs an advanced degree in economics to comprehend that the most popular programs foster the highest commercial rates and therefore generate the most revenue.

From encouraging poor eating habits and causing violence among children to corrupting politics and contributing to illiteracy, television content has been blamed for many of society's ills, and yet we can't stop watching. Many well-minded critics have yearned for more uplifting and thought-provoking programs, but the system for the most part is driven by *popularity*. Steven Bochco, the producer of such critically acclaimed television series as *Hill Street Blues*, *L.A. Law*, and *NYPD Blue*, is flattered by the adulation he has received over his career, but he is also a realist.

> Television isn't medicine; you can't prescribe it to an audience and say "You have to take this because it's good for you." That's nonsense. You like it, you watch it; you don't like it, you don't watch it. That's how it works.[2]

Program popularity is typically measured by means of national and local audience surveys conducted by Nielsen Media Research. Using a combination of electronic meters and diaries, Nielsen monitors audience behavior among random samples of households.[3] A detailed discussion of ratings research methods and usages is presented in chapter 6, but for now, our focus will be on the creation, distribution, and marketing of programs within the system of American television.

For the sake of simplicity, we will look first at programming from the standpoint of a local station. Once the reader understands this perspective, network and production company perspectives can be understood better. The final portion of this chapter recognizes two other important factors in attracting audiences, promotion and branding.

Sources of Programming

The local television station chooses from three basic sources of programming: *local*, *network*, and *syndicated*. Each offers business advantages and disadvantages for the station operator.

Local Programming

Local programming, as the name implies, originates at the local station itself. Today most local programs are newscasts, often beginning as early as 5:00 AM and continuing throughout the day at various times, concluding with a late-evening newscast at 10:00 or 11:00 PM. Aside from providing a community with much-needed information about local issues, weather, and sports, this type of local programming has proven to be highly profitable. In some cases, among large-market stations, up to 50 percent of all sales revenue can be attributed to commercials airing just in local newscasts.[4] Needless to say, this has become a hugely competitive arena, with stations investing millions of dollars in equipment, vehicles, news services, studio sets, reporters, anchors, research, and promotion.

During the past decade, locally produced newscasts have become ever more important for a station's success, not only because this type of programming can generate strong, consistent ratings, but also because stations have maximum control over costs, content, and commercials. An alternative to generating program content in-house is to purchase programs from outside companies called syndicators. As will be discussed in detail later in this chapter, owning the broadcast rights to a hit syndicated program certainly is nice, but there are trade-offs in that the broadcaster inevitably must pay increasing contract renewal costs year after year. In addition, the broadcaster has no real control over the commercial format of a syndicated program. On the contrary, locally produced programming does not hold the broadcaster hostage to exorbitant renewal fees, rigid commercial formats, or inflexible program content. The most obvious downside to going local all the time is the cost of production. Unlike networks, which can offset their costs by charging hundreds of thousands of dollars for the nationwide exposure of commercials, local stations soon reach a point of diminishing returns, where revenue from commercials cannot keep up with money spent on overly elaborate production.

All is not lost when looking at the cost of local news, in that there are certain economies of scale that enable a station to add more newscasts without adding substantial costs. In other words, doubling the number of regular newscasts doesn't come anywhere close to doubling the cost of doing business. The more newscasts a station adds to its schedule, the more cost effective the entire news operation becomes. With only a small increase in personnel and often no increase at all in equipment or station facilities, stations can add more locally produced news programming to their schedules. In many cases, time periods that traditionally were relegated to syndicated programming, such as weekdays from 5:00 to 7:00 AM, are now hosting newscasts that attract surprisingly big audiences, often surpassing the ratings delivery of the prior syndicated fare.

The downside to investing in local news is that it becomes especially expensive for stations not ranked first or second in their respective markets. Low ratings mean low commercial rates. During economic hard times, when advertising budgets decline dramatically, poorly performing stations often will cut back or eliminate local news programming altogether in favor of less expensive syndicated programming.

Syndicated Programming

Oprah, Jeopardy, Wheel of Fortune, and *Entertainment Tonight* are just a few examples of what is called *first-run syndicated programming*. In these cases the program content is produced by somebody outside of the station—a syndicator. The station purchases the *exclusive broadcast rights* for the program in its designated television market. This is a contractual agreement for a specified period of time, typically two to five years.

When the initial contract expires, and assuming the program is still popular, the station operator and the syndicator can negotiate a *renewal agreement* for several more years. If the program is a big hit, the syndicator will naturally demand a substantial increase in broadcast rights fees. If the two parties fail to come to an agreement, the program is then available to competing stations in the same market, similar to a professional athlete becoming a "free agent." This situation often leads to bidding wars, since the syndicator is essentially auctioning the program to the highest bidder. As a result, a popular syndicated program will occasionally switch stations in a market abruptly, much to the confusion of loyal audiences.

Another type of syndicated programming is called *off-network syndication*, and as the name implies, episodes of these programs have aired previously on one of the major broadcast networks before being made available in rerun syndication. Exclusive broadcast rights are sold to individual stations based not only on the number of episodes produced but also on the number of times the program will be repeated. Unlike first-run syndicated programs, in which episodes are almost always new, off-network syndication contracts typically deal with several reruns of each episode over many years. America seems never to tire of watching the same episodes of *M*A*S*H*, *The Andy Griffith Show*, *Gilligan's Island*, and *Seinfeld*. Repeat airings of an off-network program are called "runs" and can be an important factor in negotiating overall value of the program to a station. For example, the total price for owning one hundred episodes for three runs each would be less expensive than owning the same one hundred episodes for five runs each. Similar to first-run agreements, contracts between station and syndicator can be renewed or dissolved at specified times. A renewal contract can be structured quite differently than the original contract in terms of the duration of the agreement and number of runs per episode. Sometimes these off-network reruns simply "wear out" from excessive exposure, and ratings begin to decline. Under these circumstances a station may be willing to renew—but at a much lower cost and a shorter commitment. On the other hand, some off-network series somehow improve with age, resulting in some high-priced renewals.

A common but dangerous practice in the syndication business is the selling of program rights today for episodes that will not be available for airing for many years. This long-range, advanced purchasing is called *futures*, similar in concept to stock futures. In most cases futures are found among extremely popular network programs that have yet to achieve a sufficient number of episodes (usually 100) for station syndication. The risk factors are obviously high, but desperate broadcasters will often roll the dice to assure future programming needs.

The purchase of almost any syndicated program today involves not only a cash payment to the syndicator but also a so-called *barter* arrangement in which the syndicator is permitted to sell a specified number of commercials within the program to national advertisers. This commercial time cannot be used by the local station's sales department, and none of the derived revenue goes to the station. Consequently, the forfeiture of these commercial opportunities is part of the overall "cost" of the program.

When negotiating the purchase price of a syndicated program, the station must weigh several crucial factors. First, the station must predict the program's audience delivery (expected ratings) and its expected long-term performance over several years. This analysis involves looking at (a) when the program will be scheduled, (b) its lead-in and lead-out programs, and, most important, (c) the type of competition it may face from other stations during that time period. The process can be far more art than science, particularly for newly syndicated properties, in which there is little or no information on how the program has performed in similar markets. For newly released off-network programs, prior network ratings can be examined, but this is no guarantee of similar performance in station syndication. Virtually all off-network syndicated programs were scheduled in prime time, but in syndication these programs are typically scheduled in other time periods. In addition, the original programs were scheduled once a week on their respective networks, but in station syndication, they will most likely be "stripped" five days a week. The syndicated programming landscape is strewn with familiar titles, such as the giant sitcom hit *All in the Family*, that were hugely successful in prime-time network television and huge flops in local station syndication.

Based on expected audience levels, the second step is to determine how much the station can plausibly earn from owning this program, often referred to as a program's *revenue potential*. In other words, how much can the station charge for commercials? Again, this step can be more art than science, requiring a lot of educated guessing about the business climate and the competition. By multiplying the number of commercial insertion opportunities by the projected commercial rate (while remembering that the program may not be a total sellout during certain slow business months) the station management comes up with a revenue potential figure. Chapter 4, which addresses the selling of audiences to advertisers, takes a far more detailed look at the factors that influence commercial pricing and scheduling.

The third step in this evaluation process is to compare the *revenue potential* of the program with its *expected cost* (that is, the broadcast rights). Of course, this is all dependent on the program delivering its promised ratings and the economic forecasts being accurate. Nothing lowers commercial rates quite like poor ratings coupled with a bad economy!

One vital factor that must be included in the above-mentioned calculations is the number of *barter avails* given to the syndicator. Too many barter avails can interfere with the revenue potential of a program in that the station cannot take full advantage of its commercial inventory. This *barter syndication* practice began in the 1970s as a device to help lower the cash cost of syndicated programming for stations, but over the years it has mutated into a second source of impressive profits for syndicators. For television broadcasters, there is no sense of "saving money" by agreeing to this barter arrangement. Today the stations have little choice but to relinquish these avails and often pay out big cash payments to syndicators. In some instances syndicated programs take as much as 50 percent of the program's commercial inventory. Occasionally stations will negotiate a *straight barter* agreement in which no cash dollars are expended. Avails are ordinarily split 50/50.[5]

Once the genuine revenue potential of a syndicated program has been calculated, the station management can then ascertain how much the program rights are worth. One major factor influencing the final price is the size of the market. Assuming big markets can charge more for commercials and, therefore, earn more revenue than little markets, a station located in Rochester, New York, would not pay as much for broadcast rights to a syndicated program as would a station located in New York City. As mentioned earlier, the U.S. system supports approximately 210 FCC-designated television markets of varying size. Nielsen Media Research refers to these markets as Designated Market Areas or DMAs.[6]

Crazy bidding wars among stations for syndicated programming can result in distorted figures that do not necessarily correspond with market size. One can find scores of cases in which a television station paid far too much for a syndicated program that never fulfilled ratings and revenue expectations. Often these disappointing programs are rescheduled or downgraded to less important time periods, such as late-night hours, where they live in a kind of purgatory until the contract finally expires. Meanwhile, the station management desperately seeks a replacement program for the original time slot, running the same risk of becoming embroiled in another bidding war with one or more competing stations.

Many syndicated contracts contain *upgrading* and *downgrading* provisions in which the cost per episode will vary according to the time period in which the program is scheduled. For instance, if a program is rescheduled from early afternoon to late night, the broadcast rights fee would probably decrease. Conversely, if a program is highly successful in a lesser time period, and the station wants to upgrade it to a more lucrative time of day, the syndicator might demand a higher rights fee. Occasionally, syndicated contracts will stipulate certain *ratings thresholds* in which rights fees can be altered either up or down, depending on audience delivery reflected in Nielsen ratings.

Revenue Potential Exercise

Perhaps the best way to understand how revenue potential contributes to the whole negotiation process is to present a brief exercise. Suppose a station is interested in purchasing the Monday-through-Friday "strip" first-run syndicated broadcast rights to a one-hour talk show. The syndicator informs the station management that several stations in the market are also interested in bidding on the property. To open up negotiations, the syndicator states that she is asking a minimum bid of $2,000 *cash per episode* (one run) plus four thirty-second barter avails within the program over a three-year contract. The program format consists of a total of six two-minute commercial breaks, meaning each break can accommodate four thirty-second *commercial avails* for a grand total of twenty-four avails. Subtracting the four barter avails (one two-minute break) already committed to the syndicator, the local station will have access in each episode to a maximum of twenty avails to sell to advertisers.

Based on a combination of serious research and crystal ball gazing, the station management predicts that, given the current competitive program environment in the market, this program will attract at least ten thousand households to the station each day. Assuming these audience predictions are reasonably accurate, the station sales manager then estimates that the station's sales force could realistically charge on average of $200 per thirty-second commercial. Multiplying this commercial rate by twenty (the number of usable avails) results in a *daily revenue potential* of $4,000. Subtracting the per-episode cash fee going to the syndicator, in a perfect world the station would generate a profit of $2,000 each episode.

Now let us return to the bidding war. The management of our station is notified that another station has raised the per-episode cash offer to $3,000. (Note: Typically, in a bidding situation, the barter avail arrangement is seldom changed.) Should we up the ante or walk away? Here are some of the questions that must be answered quickly.

- Is a lesser profit margin still acceptable?
- Are the audience delivery predictions reliable?
- Are the commercial rate predictions reliable?
- Is there another syndicated program available that would be just as competitive but less expensive?
- What would life be like if this program were *against us* on a competing station?
- Is the other station merely bluffing, intending to artificially raise the cost of the program for us?

Finally, after much soul-searching and number-crunching, the station rolls the dice and offers $3,500 with the understanding that if the station *downgrades* the program's time period within six months, the rights fee must drop to $2,000. As this offer is put on the table, all other bidders in the market remain silent. The broadcast rights are awarded to our station, and the syndicator buys everybody dinner at an expensive restaurant.

Each year several thousand television professionals attend the National Association of Television and Programming Executives (NATPE) convention to discuss programming issues and preview new syndicated offerings. For many years deals were consummated in person at the conference, but gradually the negotiation process has moved to other venues such as station group headquarters. Many times the transaction is accomplished through e-mail, cell phones, and faxes, without the old-fashioned handshake to signal a "done deal." In addition to domestic syndication, NATPE is also a showcase for international syndication. For many syndicated programs, real profits are found in overseas markets. This is similar to the motion picture industry, where many movies barely break even in the United States but reap millions of dollars in international distribution. Substituting actor voices or "overdubbing" to accommodate different languages has become a successful cottage industry for television and movies. In addition to its annual convention, NATPE provides other resources for its members, including regional seminars, research data, and publications.[7]

Network Programming

The third major source of programming for a station is a network. As mentioned earlier, the networks themselves own several stations in large markets, but the majority of participating stations in a network are *affiliates* owned by other companies. For several decades, with only ABC, CBS, and NBC operating full-scale national networks, many stations in the United States had no network affiliation and were designated as *independent* stations, relying on local and syndicated programming to attract audiences. In recent years, the number of English-language broadcast networks has increased dramatically as well as major Spanish-language networks, such as Univision and Telemundo. The result has been fewer purely independent stations still operating in the United States.

The essential business model for a network relationship with a television station is that in exchange for airing a network's nationally distributed programming, the local affiliated station, regardless of a program's ratings, is paid a flat, monthly fee called *network compensation* (or abbreviated as "net comp"). The amount of compensation has been influenced by several variables, including the time of day, the station's ratings performance, and its record of network preemptions. Newer networks, such as Fox and the now-defunct UPN and WB networks, often paid their affiliates no compensation at all. In addition to providing exclusive programming to its designated station in each market, the network also offers a limited number of commercial avails within most programs for the station to sell to advertisers. These local commercial opportunities are called *network adjacencies* and usually command the highest commercial rates on the station. Dramatic reductions in the amount of compensation and the number of commercial adjacencies on the part of most networks in recent years have hurt the once-solid marriage between stations and networks. Chapter 8 presents a more detailed inquiry into the whole station-network relationship.

Although according to the FCC a station has the legal right to reject or *preempt* any network program on the grounds of unacceptable content, a network-affiliated station must agree in principle to broadcast or *clear* the majority of programs offered by a network. Some networks offer more programming than others. For instance, the Big Three networks (ABC, CBS, and NBC) offer far more daytime programming than the remaining smaller networks. One can look at the network relationship from two contrasting viewpoints. The good news is that the major networks provide free programming, and an affiliated station is therefore not burdened financially with having to produce local programs or purchase syndicated programs to accommodate all these unfilled hours. Furthermore, the network affiliates do not have to share in the enormous cost of creating network program content, which often surpasses $1 million per episode for a prime-time drama.[5] The bad news for stations is that there is an obvious trade-off, wherein the network gives its affiliates only a small number of commercial adjacencies, far fewer than what a station receives from investing in local or syndicated programming. The ordinary viewer is not aware that only a handful of commercials inserted within a prime-time program belong to the local station.

Similar to the way in which a station acquires the broadcast rights for syndicated programs, *network affiliation* is a contractual agreement containing a specific expiration date that requires a *renewal* procedure. In most instances over the years these procedures have been almost automatic, but there have been some cases of divorce. For example, in the 1980s, when ABC began to emerge as a viable competitor in network programming with the likes of *Charlie's Angels* and *Fantasy Island,* mass defections occurred among CBS and NBC affiliates. At the time, many ABC affiliates were struggling UHF operations, and ABC management was eager to bolster its VHF station line-up. The up-and-coming network persuaded many VHF NBC and CBS affiliates, when it was time for their renewals, to abandon their long-standing relationships and join the ABC family of stations. Of course, ABC had to use more than its enormously popular prime-time programs to lure stations to switch networks. They also offered huge cash compensation packages that often were two to three times bigger than the fees paid by CBS and NBC at the time.[8]

The 1990s witnessed a similar affiliation shake-up when Fox began to make serious inroads against the entrenched Big Three with edgy, youth-oriented programs such as *The Simpsons* and *Married with Children* and snatching away the network broadcast rights to NFL football from CBS. Again, the challenger network wanted to discard its poorly performing, mostly UHF-affiliated stations in favor of more powerful VHF stations. Similar to the ABC strategy, Fox encouraged station defections by offering not only attractive programming but huge cash compensation packages. When the dust finally settled in the mid 1990s, dozens of stations throughout the United States had switched network affiliation to Fox.[9]

Switching network affiliation has a compounding effect in most markets in that one switch inevitably motivates additional switches. For example, having lost an affiliated station to a competing network, the abandoned network will be looking for a new affiliate in the market. This usually involves the network approaching not only independent stations but also affiliates of competing networks. Often a station that is disenchanted with its current network relationship can be persuaded to jump ship—especially if the price is right. Such a move then sets the stage for yet another network switch among the remaining stations in a market.

Although network compensation is certainly a good thing for a station's coffers, far more revenue is generated from selling commercial adjacencies. One nagging problem alluded to earlier is that adjacencies are few in number. That is, the vast majority of commercials seen within a network program are exclusive network commercials in which the affiliated stations share none of the revenue. For example, within a typical prime-time network program, approximately fifteen minutes are given over to commercials, of which only two minutes may be available to the local station affiliate to sell. As with the restrictions surrounding barter avails within syndicated programs, network affiliates cannot take full advantage of the commercial inventory found in network programs. Unlike first-run and off-network syndicated programs that typically require significant cash outlays by a station, network programming is acquired essentially free from the parent network, and the networks are therefore not overly generous in providing commercial avails for local station use (adjacencies). The networks instead argue that because they assume all the production costs and rights fees for creating this expensive programming, they deserve to control most of the commercial inventory.

Some industry observers are confused by the fact that many network programs that go into off-network syndication end up on stations with a completely different network affiliation. For example, *Seinfeld*, after many successful seasons on NBC, became available for station syndication. Around the country, stations affiliated not only with NBC but all other networks bid on the program with the intention of stripping it in the afternoon or late-night time periods.

Beginning in the 1970s and continuing through 1994, the FCC had enforced a Financial Interest and Syndication Ruling (often abbreviated as the Fin-Syn Rules) forbidding American networks from having a financial interest in the production or eventual syndication of a network program.[10] At the time, the commission and Congress were worried about the powerful control the three networks exerted over the creation and distribution of program content. The Fin-Syn Rules attempted to dilute this power by forcing the networks to purchase programs from independent studios and production companies that retained ownership of the program property, including the right to syndicate the program on a station level. With the introduction of new multi-channel media options, such as cable, satellite, and the Internet, offering hundreds of program choices, rather than just three, as was the case in the 1970s when the rule was made, the networks eventually persuaded the FCC to rescind the rules. Now the networks create considerable programming "in-house" and participate in syndication. A recent example is *Everybody Loves Raymond*, in which CBS-Viacom invested in both the production and off-network syndication of the program.

Some group-owned stations participate in programming that is a kind of hybrid between local and syndicated. These are productions produced by the group owner itself and distributed to its member stations. This is most common among network-owned-and-operated (O&O) stations where the parent company owns or has investments in production companies, movie studios, and syndication firms. For example, in the program schedule for WTVJ displayed below, the program airing at 11:00 AM, *Starting Over*, is a product of NBC Enterprises, the station syndication subsidiary of corporate parent NBC Universal. For the first year, all NBC-owned stations carried the in-house "syndicated" program. From a strict accounting perspective, these stations did provide license fees to offset production costs, but obviously all the money is kept within the financial walls of the parent corporation, ultimately contributing to corporate earnings and resulting stock values. *Starting Over* has since expanded into the general syndication market, making itself available to dozens of television markets not serviced by an NBC O&O station. Unlike conventional syndication rules of the game, if the program is a hit, the NBC O&Os will not be held ransom by the syndicator for ever-increasing renewal fees. Since each of the major networks owns dozens of stations in major cities, particularly top-ten markets such as New York, Los Angeles, Chicago, Boston, and Philadelphia, this *in-house* syndicated programming business strategy is a shrewd way to reap the best of both worlds.

A Typical Broadcast Day

A network-affiliated television station will make use of all three sources of programming—local, syndicated, and network. The table below reveals program sources for a typical broadcast day at NBC Miami affiliate WTVJ in 2006.

WTVJ Program Schedule and Sources of Content		
Time period	Program	Program source
6:00-7:00 AM	Local newscast	Local
7:00-10:00 AM	Today Show	Network
10:00-11:00 AM	South Florida Today	Local
11:00-Noon	Starting Over	Syndicated
Noon-12:30 PM	Ambush Makeover	Syndicated
12:30-1:00 PM	Celebrity Justice	Syndicated
1:00-2:00 PM	Days of Our Lives	Network
2:00-3:00 PM	Passions	Network
3:00-4:00 PM	People's Court	Syndicated
4:00-5:00 PM	Ellen DeGeneres	Syndicated
5:00-6:30 PM	Various local newscasts	Local
6:30-7:00 PM	NBC Nightly News	Network
7:00-7:30 PM	Extra	Syndicated
7:30-8:00 PM	Access Hollywood	Syndicated
8:00-11:00 PM	Various NBC prime time	Network
11:00-11:30 PM	Local newscast	Local
11:30-Midnight	Tonight with Jay Leno	Network

Notice in the WTVJ schedule that the station changes program sources several times during the course of a broadcast day. Although the average viewer probably is not aware of these shifts, the station management is more than aware of the business implications of such changes. In terms of managing costs, content, and commercials, each of these program sources presents unique advantages and disadvantages for a local station.

Dealing with network programming also has its ups and downs for a station. Although there is no serious cash dispersed by the station, a network affiliate has restricted commercial opportunities and little if any control over program content. In addition, all networks hope to phase out compensation fees in the next few years. These and other frustrations emanating from the station-network relationship are discussed in more detail in later chapters.

The Network Perspective

Now that we have a basic understanding of programming options and consequences from a local-station perspective, we are ready to change hats and imagine that we are now network program executives sitting in our plush offices overlooking the skyline of New York or L.A. Just like local stations, networks are in the business of selling audiences to advertisers using programming as a means of attracting national audiences. In order to distribute programs nationwide, the networks use a combination of stations that they own plus dozens more *affiliated stations* owned by other broadcasters located around the country.

Networks acquire programming from studios and production companies, some of which may be owned by the network's parent company. Giant media mergers, such as Disney with ABC and Universal with NBC, are intended to keep both program production and distribution under one roof. But many programs are still obtained from outside producers.

From Network Pilot to Off-Network Syndication: The Case Study of *Seinfeld*

Examining the life and times of the hit sitcom *Seinfeld* offers a good case study in the complexities of network programming and how popular programs enter off-network syndication.

Step 1: Pilot development

Jerry Seinfeld and some business partners conjure up a great idea for a network sitcom "about nothing." They hire a production company, an unforgettable ensemble of actors, and a group of talented writers to create a half-hour pilot program to be evaluated by executives at the NBC network. Today, most program proposals require an initial script *approval* before entering into genuine production of a pilot.

Step 2: Program acceptance

After much deliberation and audience testing, NBC makes an offer to purchase the network broadcast rights for thirteen original episodes, with the understanding that if the program's ratings achieve a certain threshold, the network will request additional episodes to round out the season. Today, for many new programs this initial order has shrunk from thirteen to six episodes. Because it is an untried program featuring a relatively unknown cast, the network licensing fee paid to Jerry and his colleagues is modest. New programs often must endure *deficit financing*, meaning that the network does not pay the producers sufficient funds to completely offset the initial cost of production. The program producers usually assume the risk, hoping the program will beat the odds and have a long run on the network followed by continued success in off-network syndication. Because most network programs fail in their first or second year, obliterating any chance of serious syndication opportunities, deficit financing is not for the financially squeamish.

Step 3: The program survives its first season

After a slow start, the program catches on with audiences and television critics. By the end of the first season *Seinfeld* is on the verge of becoming a hit. Jerry Seinfeld and his partners negotiate a new contract for its second season. This time they ask for a lot more money—no more deficit financing! NBC agrees.

Step 4: The program year after year ranks number one in prime time

As the program continues to make broadcast history with classic episodes such as "The Soup Nazi," "The Contest," and "Yadda, Yadda," NBC is forced to pay ever-increasing licensing fees, eventually reaching millions of dollars per episode. Of course, the network charges staggeringly high commercial rates to advertisers eager to be in the show. Consequently, the program still generates a handsome profit for the network, at least until its final two years.

Step 5: The program goes into syndication while remaining on NBC

After creating approximately one hundred episodes, most successful network programs go into off-network syndication, where local stations on a market-by-market basis purchase the exclusive broadcast rights to air reruns. *Seinfeld* followed the typical pattern, producing new episodes for NBC and selling old episodes in syndication. Because there are no new production costs, off-network syndication of popular programs is extremely profitable for Mr. Seinfeld and friends. By having the program available in almost every television market in the country, the syndicator then begins to sell barter commercial avails to national advertisers. Meanwhile, the newly minted episodes are airing in prime time on NBC. Now Jerry Seinfeld is making money from (a) ongoing NBC network licensing fees, (b) off-network syndication fees, and (c) barter commercials imbedded within the syndicated episodes. Each year, the most recent network episodes are placed into the syndication packages. Life is good, and it gets even better in a few years.

Step 6: Seinfeld calls it quits, but the program lives on

After nine years, the *Seinfeld* crew agrees to stop while they are at the top of their game, much to the distress of NBC, although the show's license fees for the final two years are extraordinarily high for the network. Many stations carrying the program in syndication eagerly negotiate contract renewals at higher prices than those achieved from the first cycle of reruns. Instead of wearing out, *Seinfeld* episodes seem immune to overexposure.

In 1998 the program strikes gold again when the TBS cable network purchases all episodes. Coined *cable syndication* rather than broadcast syndication, this business venture, although perfectly legal, causes some frustration among conventional television stations that paid dearly for the exclusive *broadcast rights* but not exclusive *cable rights* to the program. That is, the contracted stations are protected from another television station in the same market airing the program but not from a national cable network providing the same programming to a local cable system servicing the same market. Consequently, audiences in almost every television market can see reruns of *Seinfeld* each night on local television and on cable. Once again, ordinary viewers probably do not comprehend (or care about) the technological economic and regulatory differences between the two versions of *Seinfeld*.

Why Networks Prefer to Produce In-house

Returning to step 1 of our *Seinfeld* case study, NBC at the beginning was getting a bargain with its business relationship with the program producers, but as the show became an enormous hit, the cost of doing business for the network escalated dramatically. Furthermore, after a long, successful run in prime time, NBC could not share in the program's syndication profits. In a perfect world, if NBC could go back in time, it would have owned the program outright, or at least been an equity partner with Seinfeld. Of course, ownership brings risk. With most new television programs getting cancelled within a couple of years, there is something to be said for remaining a "renter" rather than an owner. Still, almost half of all prime-time programs today have a network as an owner or partner.[11]

Types of Program Content

Program content has changed dramatically since television's inception in the 1940s, but the intention of this book is not to be a time traveler, exploring sixty years of broadcasting nostalgia. Instead, we will concentrate on the current trends, emphasizing the underlying business elements. Today the following categories seem to accommodate the majority of programs currently available, in station syndication or on one of the broadcast networks.

- Drama
- Sitcom
- Newscast
- News Magazine
- Talk Show
- Live Sports
- Soaps
- Game Shows
- Reality

Of course, one will always find a breakthrough program that seems to defy easy categorization. In 2005 *Desperate Housewives* became a huge hit, yet audiences and media observers debated whether its dark humor was comedy or drama. Similarly, the term "reality" programming seems overly broad if all *non-scripted* content is to be ascribed to this singular category. That is, should programs such as *American Idol* and *Survivor* be regarded as within the same genre? Categorizing cable programming is even more exasperating. Rather than splitting hairs over the definitions from a creative standpoint, this author prefers to approach the challenge from the vantage point of business and economics.

The Program Producer's View

We will now change hats and take a brief look at the producers' perspective, the people who create "the product" for distribution. Regardless of a program's type or genre, the producer of a new endeavor has three choices for distribution: network, station syndication, or cable. These options are not necessarily mutually exclusive. Over time, repeat episodes of a successful network program can migrate to off-network station syndication and possibly move again to cable. Hit shows such as *Seinfeld, Friends,* and *Everybody Loves Raymond* have acquired this triple exposure. Sometimes programs enter first-run syndication after the idea has been rejected by broadcast and cable networks. On the other hand, some programs from the very beginning have been intended for station syndication. In general, programs intending to be *stripped* five days a week usually head for syndication rather than network distribution, simply because the networks have so few opportunities for new entries of this type. Conversely, once-per-week programs tend to be produced for broadcast and cable networks rather than syndication simply because local stations have so few opportunities for new entries of this type.

One important principle that all producers must consider is what we will call the program's potential *repeat capacity*. That is, some types of programs have little or no afterlife, while others can prosper for decades in rerun heaven. This capacity can have a profound influence on how a producer calculates the long-term costs and benefits of creating a program. For many network programs, the only way producers and production companies earn substantial profits has been through reruns in syndication. In recent years, however, this premise has been disrupted by non-scripted "reality" programs that seldom, if ever, go into off-network syndication. With little hope of "back end" syndication rights, the producers must profit immediately. Consequently, producers are rejecting the old deficit-financing schemes based on future repeat capacity. Occasionally, the most popular reality programs get a brief second life when they are *repurposed* for perhaps one added exposure (or run) on cable. Similarly, producers of first-run syndicated programming know that continued success means continued production of fresh product, with no long-term opportunities for reruns. Unlike the producers of off-network rerun hits, such as *M*A*S*H*, who have reaped millions, while never creating a single new episode, the producers of most first-run syndicated hits must replenish their highly perishable program content five nights a week. Game shows such as *Jeopardy* and *Wheel of Fortune*, talk shows such as *Oprah* and *Ellen DeGeneres*, entertainment magazines such as *Entertainment Tonight* and *Access Hollywood*, do not have the capacity to be repeated again and again for years to come. As with network reality programming, producers of first-run syndicated programming require immediate profits. If the program remains a hit on a network or station, the producers can get rich by negotiating ever-higher license fees. But as soon as the program is cancelled or goes out of production for other reasons, there is no future in reruns. Millions of people will watch twenty-year-old episodes of *M*A*S*H*, but who will watch a twenty-year-old episode of *Entertainment Tonight?*

Instead of station syndication, some program producers, especially creators of one-hour dramas such as the ubiquitous *Law and Order* and its several clones, opt for what has been called *cable syndication*. Semantics become a problem here, because the definition of the term syndication has been broadened to include not only local television stations but also cable networks. Essentially, cable syndication occurs when a program moves from a broadcast network to a cable network. Often this move occurs while the original broadcast network program is still on the air with freshly produced episodes. Furthermore, the same program may also be in station syndication. For instance, there was a period when brand-new episodes of *Friends* could be viewed on NBC at the same time that rerun episodes could be seen in syndication on hundreds of local stations and on the TBS cable network.

The Art and Science of Scheduling

People watch television for all kinds of reasons. Television programmers have long been aware of the capacity of a program to "inherit" sizable audiences from the program scheduled immediately before it—its *lead-in*. That is, audience choice sometimes appears to be the result of clever scheduling rather than compelling content. Although intervening factors such as program genre, the lead-out program, and time of day have been shown to have some minor influence on this phenomenon, by far the most powerful predictor of program ratings has been the size of a program's lead-in audience. This phenomenon has been called "inheritance effects" or "lead-in effects."[12]

One might think that with the introduction of so many program choices from cable, satellite, and even the Internet, the long-standing power of lead-in effects would be on the decline, but empirical research disagrees. Despite all these new choices, lead-in programming on broadcast television remains a potent force.

Television programmers have come up with several scheduling strategies that take advantage not only of the show but also the flow. Over the years, these program-scheduling strategies have acquired their own special jargon. For example, placing a relatively weak or unfamiliar program between two strong programs is called *hammocking*. This is a common strategy used to stimulate sampling of a new program. Inserting a strong program between two weaker entries has been dubbed *tent-poling* and is often associated with the notion of salvaging a poor program line-up. Offering several adjacent programs with highly similar content, such as an evening of sitcoms, is called *block programming*. The strategy of responding to a competitor with radically different program content is known as *counter-programming*.[13]

The creation of program content that is aimed at a relatively specialized audience has been called *niche programming* and is far more common within the cable industry than within broadcasting. Television programmers, for the most part, have shunned the niche approach, preferring to go after larger, heterogeneous audience groups.

Regulation of Television Content

As will be discussed in greater detail in chapter 5, broadcasting is regulated by the government far more than other media. In addition to assigning station licenses, allocating frequencies and channels, and enforcing engineering guidelines concerning operating, power, antenna height, and signal clarity, the FCC has a history of becoming involved in prescribing content. Although always encouraging competition and the free market, the commission has often imposed controversial restrictions and requirements on television content. For the creative community, including producers, writers, directors, and actors, the most exasperating government regulations have centered on the notion of *indecency*, which is strictly a radio and television problem. Creators of cable programming have so far been exempt from any FCC indecency prosecution. This free pass has allowed cable to explore more mature and provocative topics without fear of government censorship.

Promotion and Branding

In addition to using program content to attract audiences, stations and networks also make use of marketing communications to persuade audiences to try a new program and to alert audiences to the upcoming content of their favorite programs. One might see some irony in the fact that advertising media such as radio and television spend millions of dollars advertising themselves on other media. For example, a local station typically will buy advertising in newspapers, magazines, radio, cable, and billboards, all of which are competitors!

Within the television industry, the marketing of programs to audiences has traditionally been called *promotion*, although in recent years stations have adopted *marketing* or *creative services* to denote the same function. Many operations divide responsibilities between *audience promotion* aimed at potential viewers and *sales promotion* aimed at potential advertisers.[14]

Although market stations and the national networks have sizable budgets to win the hearts and minds of audiences, their most important asset is their own air time. Commercials promoting one's own programming are called *promos* and are produced and scheduled in the same manner as real commercials, only these announcements are free. Furthermore, most broadcast networks are involved with "sister" cable networks owned by the same parent corporation, enabling not only the repurposing of program content but also what is called *cross-promotion*, whereby the networks air promos for each other. For example, NBC News often cross-promotes programming on MSNBC cable, or ABC Sports often promotes ESPN talent and programming. This practice infuriates network-affiliated stations not owned by the parent company. From their perspective, the network is in a sense driving audiences away from their stations. The networks are not particularly sympathetic, because these audiences are merely pushed to another media subsidiary of the parent operation.

Branding and many of the notions of brand management are not new to most American consumer goods. Some of today's most prominent brands, such as Coke, Levi, Maxwell House, Budweiser, Campbell, and Kellogg, began their branding efforts in the 1880s when electronic media wasn't an industry or even an idea. What is new, however, is the adoption of branding and brand management by the electronic media. Radio and television broadcasters have for decades given unique "brand names" to their stations, networks, and programs, but the decade of the 1990s introduced a much deeper interest in the art and science of brand management.[15]

The primary motivation for applying brand management to a consumer product or service is competition. As the number of similar products or services in the marketplace increases, the need for highly differentiated brands becomes more important. The late arrival of brand management to American television was due primarily to a lack of competition. For over three decades, the competitive arena for commercial television was restricted to three major players: ABC, CBS, and NBC. With so few stations licensed to each market, viewer choices were restricted to a handful of media brands. By the late 1980s, the competitive picture began to change when cable took off, offering dozens more viewing options.

Brand management has a special role within the larger context of promotion. Some promotion activities may have a branding component, while others may not. In simple terms, branding deals with a product's *reputation*. This encompasses those promotion activities that are intended to distinguish a brand from its competitors by communicating to consumers what the brand stands for. What is important to remember here is that, despite the use of all of these marketing tools, promoting isn't always *branding*. For example, a program's ratings success may be more the result of clever program scheduling or transitory promotion hype rather than genuine audience preference for the program. Does a "Watch and Win" contest generate audience sampling or merely short-lived audience traffic that disappears as soon as the contest ends? After the sweeps, will the program sustain its high ratings, or will they sink like a rock? Effective media branding strategies are designed for the long run.

Although there are dozens of definitions of brand equity offered by academia and the private sector, all experts would agree that equity stems from the added value a brand name contributes to a product's performance in the marketplace. For television broadcasters, performance means ratings and revenue. At times the broadcast networks have been accused of abandoning their brand imagery for the short-terms gains of a quick ratings hit, not worrying if it meshes well with an established brand identity. ABC marketing chief Mike Benson realizes that "Everybody wants to grow their audience. We're all in the game of getting the most eyeballs because it's all about ratings. But I think you do ideally need to stand for something."[16]

Networks, stations, producers, syndicators, and marketers are all part of the dynamic system intended to attract audiences. The next step is to take these captured audiences and *sell* them to advertisers.

Questions and Exercises

1   If you were a program producer with a great idea for a new show, which content distributor would you "pitch" first: a broadcast network or a first-run syndication company? Explain your reasons why.

2   Suppose you were a network executive evaluating several *pilot* scripts for next season. What factors would you consider most important for success?

3   *Lead-in* programming has been proven to be important to the ratings success of many prime-time programs. Find a copy of tonight's television listings and identify programs that you suspect are especially dependent on their lead-ins.

4   Following up on question #3, the *scheduling* of programs has been considered to be both art and science. Returning to your television listings, analyze audience attraction not only from lead-in programming but also in relationship to direct *competition* on other broadcast networks.

5   Can you explain why some hit network television shows perform poorly in syndication (such as *All in the Family*) while others flourish in reruns for decades (such as *M*A*S*H*)?

The Bottom Line

Selling Audiences to Advertisers

Television pioneer and comedian Milton Berle one night asked his wife, "Do you feel the sex and excitement has gone out of our marriage?" She answered, "I'll discuss it with you during the next commercial."[1]

Commercials: we love them, hate them, tolerate them, embrace them, and sometimes *zap* them. After more than a half century of "Where's the beef?," "You deserve a break today," "You're in good hands," "Just do it," and "What's in your wallet?," virtually everybody knows what a television commercial is, but many people do not have a comprehensive understanding of the underlying business model and how it came into existence. We will begin this chapter by examining the most fundamental aspects of the model and then progress to more complex subtopics.

Advertising

Advertising is the fuel that makes the engine of commercial broadcasting run. The basic assumption of all advertising is that properly composed and distributed messages can influence people's attitudes and behavior. Some advertising is intended merely to create awareness of a particular brand and generate a positive image, while more ambitious advertising strategies attempt to motivate people to act on this knowledge by purchasing a product or service. With the advent of political advertising, the desired "purchase" is someone's vote. Regardless of the type of items for sale or the persuasion techniques used, media provide the *bridge* between a business and its intended customers. Advertisers can choose from a vast array of media, including local and national television. Advertising professionals realize that, depending on the needs of their client, some media work better than others. For example, print media, such as newspapers and magazines, have the obvious advantage of allowing an advertiser to express relatively long, complex messages requiring considerable time to comprehend (for instance, a detailed listing of fifty automobiles for sale by a local dealer providing unique features, options, and price).

On the other hand, other media, particularly television, can use emotional and symbolic techniques that print media cannot come close to replicating (for example, using color, motion, and sound to imbue a brand of automobile with sex appeal). From its earliest beginnings, television has been a powerful advertising tool.

Some Background

When radio broadcasting was in its infancy in the 1920s, this notion of commercial advertising was not a sure thing. For decades print media, such as newspapers and magazines, had been private enterprises using subscriptions or advertising as a means to make money, but with the introduction of the new medium of radio, some concerned citizens and government officials believed that it should be nonprofit and operated by the government with no intervention from the private sector. This attitude was soon displaced by aggressive entrepreneurs who advocated the more familiar capitalistic business model utilized by print media, that is, private ownership and permission to run the endeavor as a business.[1] In addition, the First Amendment to the U.S. Constitution, guaranteeing freedom of expression, had become an important and staunchly defended component of American culture. Indeed, "commercial speech" today is accepted and protected by the high courts as an integral part of free speech.[2] Unlike most of the rest of the world, which created broadcast systems with considerably more government involvement, the founders of the U.S. broadcasting industry set the tone for the early development of what we call today commercial television.

Of course, government could not be excluded completely from the introduction of broadcasting because of technological issues that could not be ignored. Unlike the print media, broadcasters had to deal with (a) a scarcity of available frequencies from which a station could operate and (b) a nagging problem of signal interference in which stations in the same market were broadcasting on the identical frequency, resulting in neither station being heard at all by audiences. These structural issues, grounded in the laws of physics, opened the door for some degree of government oversight. The role of government, and particularly the Federal Communications Commission (FCC), will be discussed in chapter 6. For now, while the discussion is focused on the basic business model, the reader should understand that, unlike much of the rest of the world, the American system of broadcasting has always been regarded as a private *business*.

The very first attempts at applying an advertising-based business model to radio were a far cry from today's familiar thirty-second or sixty-second commercial. The first advertising announcements were relatively long scripts intended to persuade people to buy radios sets. The thinking then was that the "business" of radio would be the retail purchase of new radios sets. The actual broadcasts were seen merely as a marketing device to get people to buy the necessary listening appliance. As radio became ever more popular, the demand for radio sets would escalate dramatically. Several years would pass before a handful of businesses other than radio manufacturers decided to test the waters and try to sell a product or service. According to several historians, the first such advertisement occurred in 1922 when a New Jersey real-estate developer purchased ten minutes of air time to persuade the audience to visit a new suburban housing development. Moments after the broadcast, the realtor was overwhelmed with phone calls and curious visitors, and, as the saying goes, the rest is history.[3] Hundreds of different categories of products and services began to embrace the notion of reaching potential customers by purchasing air time on radio. Program *sponsorships* became a common means of integrating a client's brand directly into the program content, but this became impractical as more businesses wanted to get on the air with their messages. The broadcasters soon realized that far more money could be made if they abandoned exclusive sponsorships in favor of periodic interruptions within the program content called "breaks," featuring relatively short, standardized units of purchased time called "commercials." Additionally, advertisers soon saw a certain wisdom in being able to advertise on several programs, reaching a broader audience. This basic structure for accommodating advertisers, introduced and nurtured during 1930s and '40s, remained essentially unchanged for the next half century. Of course, the production elements and creative strategies have changed radically for commercial content, but the broadcast program architecture of specified breaks containing clusters of individual commercials is as old as *Amos and Andy* or *The Lone Ranger.*

Another important component of this transition from pure sponsorships to today's commercial break structure was a dramatic change in who produced the program content. Under the sponsorship model, the clients and their advertising agencies not only inserted advertising messages but actually produced the programming. In most cases, the radio networks essentially were distributors with little influence over program scripts or talent. The shift away from sponsorships to what has been called a "participating" spot advertising structure coincided with the networks' taking back control of their program content. Surprisingly, when television was first introduced, the notion of network program sponsorships returned for a short time, with advertising agencies once again assuming the dual roles of advertiser and producer. A series of quiz show scandals in the late 1950s, however, prompted the networks to discourage these powerful sponsorships and adopt the participating commercial structure. Sponsorships still exist today on a limited scale, usually featuring several sponsors with no direct authority over program content.

Another important development that intertwines technology, regulation, and economics was the early development of *networks* as an integral part of the broadcast industry. Radio station operators quickly realized the economic benefits of distributing programming nationwide. NBC, under the leadership of David Sarnoff, is credited with being the first company organized solely to operate a broadcasting network. Later, William Paley would transform what he called "a patchwork, money-losing little company" into the mighty CBS network.[4] By taking advantage of national networks, major national advertisers had the opportunity to reach millions of people across the country at the same time. Expensive program content, such as live broadcasts from New York and Hollywood, featuring huge orchestras and well-known performers, could be made available to the most remote communities served by the smallest of radio-station operators. In addition to airing quality programs that no single station could ever afford to produce, these stations, called network *affiliates,* were given the opportunity to insert a specified number of local commercials from which to generate revenue and, it was hoped, a profit. This became a classic example of a "win-win" or synergistic relationship, in which the networks and local stations benefited from each other. The interconnection technology was developed quickly. The FCC saw no reason to license the networks per se, because they were essentially content providers for individually licensed stations. National advertisers were more than willing to pay high rates for network-distributed commercials, thereby offsetting the costs of producing elaborate programming. Local advertisers were thrilled to have their commercials placed within the context of nationally recognized programs. A local hardware store in Rochester, New York, could air a commercial message that would be inserted into *The Jack Benny Show*. When television came on the scene, the development of television networks was only a matter of time.

Although television was in many respects something excitingly new, it was also the extension of the already-established radio industry that, through trial and error, had created a successful business model that accommodated regulatory and technological issues. For example, by the late 1940s, when television was truly coming into its own, any debate over the ownership and licensing of television stations had long been resolved. In addition, most technical challenges involving frequency, power, and interference had already been anticipated by the FCC, thanks to the agency's long experience with radio. Furthermore, the integration of advertising messages into a program structure featuring predetermined interruptions for commercials was established and flourishing on radio, only now there would be pictures as well as sound! Except for a few technological factors unique to television, the fundamental business and regulatory elements of the television industry were cloned from radio. In fact, most of the early pioneers of television were seasoned radio operators. The network giants CBS, NBC, and ABC all made the transition from radio to television.

An alternative to the advertising-based model has been direct audience support, or *pay radio* and *pay television*, both of which failed miserably. The core concept was that in exchange for commercial-free broadcasting, the audience would pay a monthly fee enabling them to decode electronically scrambled content (similar to subscribing to one of today's premium cable channels, such as HBO). While these ventures never took hold, America's current transition to multi-cast digital transmission has some entrepreneurs talking about the possibility of introducing subscriber-based television that would cater to specialized niche audiences.

The Notion of the Niche

In the early days of both radio and television, audiences were attracted because of the simple novelty of the new technology. The mere fact that pictures could be transmitted through the air to someone's home was motivation enough to purchase a set and watch just about anything. But soon, as more stations and networks came into being, audiences became more selective. Media observers noticed that some programs appeared to be more popular than others, particularly among certain demographic groupings. Instead of attempting to be all things to all people, broadcasters have been forced over the decades to narrow their goals and try to sat-isfy the needs and wants of target audiences. No doubt, the major broad-cast networks can still attract relatively large "mass audiences," but with the recent dramatic expansion of cable and satellite offerings, conventional television broadcasters on both a local and network level are beginning to focus on narrow *target audiences.* The advertising industry has responded positively to this phenomenon in that most goods and services also address targeted customers. Consequently, for many advertisers, reaching a huge mass audience is not always the answer. Instead, they are more than will-ing to purchase commercial time within programs that attract a certain *type* of audience. In order to survive in a highly competitive marketplace, most advertiser-based media have embraced the notion of *the niche.* In fact, several media scholars, most notably John Dimmick, have explored the intertwined audience-advertiser relationship as a "theory of the niche."[5] In essence, the theory maintains that in order to compete and prosper in a crowded media marketplace, individual firms must differentiate them-selves from their competitors by creating unique and desirable niches. Unlike most cable networks, which concentrate on fairly narrow content niches, such as MTV, ESPN, CNN, and Spike, broadcast television stations and networks tend to take a much wider cut by offering a variety of program niches throughout the broadcast day. For example, returning to the sta-tion program schedule presented in chapter 3, we can readily see that the target audiences change over time. Prime-time programming typically offers advertisers an even broader array of audiences to purchase. Some critics accuse the major broadcast networks of "blurring their brand identity" and risking long-term damage in establishing a recognizable niche in the minds of audiences and advertisers.[6] The broadcasters are under-standably reluctant to reduce the number of audience options available to media buyers. For instance, a typical network-affiliated television sta-tion can offer advertisers young mothers with daytime soap operas and young single men with weekend sports—alternatives that few cable net-works can provide.

Types of Television Advertising

Television advertising can be categorized four ways: *local, network, national spot,* and *syndicated barter.* You probably notice that these terms are highly similar to the terminology used to describe the different types of televi-sion *programming* found in chapter 3. This chapter merely changes our orientation so that we can better appreciate the system of commercial broad-casting. Instead of looking at this topic from the vantage point of a typical station, we will change hats once again and assume for a while that we are an advertiser.

- *Local advertising* is defined as commercials placed by a direct client or advertising agency located in the same market as the television station. For example, a local Miami car dealer purchases commercial time on a television station licensed to the Miami-Fort Lauderdale market. Commercials can be placed within local, syndicated, or network programming broadcast by the station.

- *Network advertising* is defined as commercials placed by major advertisers on the broadcast networks for national distribution. Although the commercials will be seen on hundreds of stations (network affiliates) in local markets, the stations themselves do not share in any of the commercial revenue. As mentioned earlier in this book, as part of the affiliation agreement, the networks do offer their stations the opportunity to insert local commercials called *adjacencies*.

- *National spot advertising* is defined as commercials purchased from local stations by national advertisers. That is, these national advertisers bypass the networks and go directly to individual stations. Typically a *national rep firm* acts as an intermediary or broker between an advertising agency and the station. National spot is used by national advertisers that do not want national distribution (Why air commercials for snow shovels in Florida?) or want to place special emphasis on specific markets (for example, run commercials for Florida vacation destinations in New England markets during February). For many large-market television stations, national spot dollars account for half or more of all sales revenue taken in during the year.[7]

- *Barter syndication* advertising is defined as commercials placed by national advertisers inside various syndicated programs airing on local television stations around the country. As presented in our discussion of programming, the local stations do not share in this revenue. An advertiser using this method must realize that, unlike network advertising, a specific syndicated program may not currently air in every market in the United States. Also, the advertiser cannot be assured that the program airs at the same time of day in every market where it is cleared for broadcast. The actual insertion of this type of commercial is seldom done by the station. In most cases, by the time a syndicated episode is sent via satellite to a local station for airing, these barter commercials have already been placed within the program. Of course, the station can still sell the remaining open avails to local advertisers or national spot clients.

Today, most stations are members of the Television Bureau of Advertising, commonly referred to as the TVB. This not-for-profit trade association provides members with a variety of research and sales training resources. Although some items are available only to paying members, others are available free to interested advertisers and the general public.[8]

A Closer Look at Commercial Pricing and Inventory Control

Now that we have a better understanding of the origins of the advertising-based business model and the different types of television advertising, it is appropriate to take a closer look at the art and science of commercial pricing and inventory control. By pricing we mean assigning a monetary value to specified units of commercial time embedded within programming. For each program, the total number of available units—called *avails*—that can be sold is known as the program's commercial *inventory*. Because these units are interruptions within program content, there is a threshold beyond which audiences supposedly will no longer tolerate these intrusions and change channels. Therefore, the inventory is *limited*, although in recent years the commercial threshold has increased dramatically. People's tolerance for ever more commercials seems endless.

The surrounding *program content* is time-bound by air date and time of day. As a result, the program's commercial inventory is not only limited but also perishable. Similar to an airliner with limited seating that must adhere to a flight schedule, broadcast sales managers must face the daily dilemma of "filling the seats" of their various program inventories with commercials. The challenge is to determine how much to charge before chasing away customers to a competitor. This balancing of inventory and pricing to achieve maximum revenue has been called *yield management* and is a sophisticated application of the basic economic principles of supply and demand. In simple terms, yield management is market-driven pricing in which the critical factor is to anticipate demand long before the day of the broadcast. In order to accommodate fluctuations in demand, broadcasters have historically preferred to use a flexible rather than a fixed commercial "rate card." An in-depth discussion of broadcast yield management is beyond the scope of this book, but interested readers can find fairly easy-to-comprehend information from the National Association of Broadcasters.[9]

Living in the Future

Because most commercial avails on radio and television are sold weeks, if not months, ahead of actual air dates, the buyers and sellers of media are always living in the future. Managers examine records of past activity to bolster the reliability of business forecasts. Indeed, there is a certain predictability to advertising demand in that toy stores will always want to attract shoppers for Christmas, and Disney World will always want to attract vacationers during the summer, but many other intervening factors make prognostication something less than a hard science.

For large market stations and networks, the broadcaster essentially promises a certain minimum audience delivery reflected in Nielsen ratings. If, in fact, the program or daypart does not deliver what was promised, the broadcaster is then obligated to compensate for this shortfall by offering additional free commercials called "make-goods" (that is, making good on a promise). Obviously, make-goods intrude on the current inventory of avails intended to be sold to cash customers.

Because broadcast sales executives are always living in the future, their companies operate according to an *accrual* accounting structure in which anticipated commercial deals (signed contracts) are booked as *accounts receivable*, even though the actual billing to the advertiser has yet to occur. Furthermore, sales commissions are not awarded until the money has been collected, which might take thirty to sixty days after receipt of the bill.

Four Basic Steps

For small markets, the essential steps in consummating a buyer-seller media transaction can be rather informal. A retail shop owner and a station sales representative may negotiate a deal over a cup of coffee, with little or no discussion of ratings and statistical cost efficiencies. Large television markets and networks, however, tend to have more formal transactions that follow certain protocols and rely heavily on data. The following are four basic steps used by major advertisers and media.

1   The advertiser submits a *request for avails* informing the network or station of the desired target audience, size of budget, and airdates of campaign. In addition, buyers may stipulate desired *gross ratings points*, audience *reach*, and *frequency* goals. These items will be described in more detail in chapter 6.

2   The network or station responds to these requests with a proposed *sales plan* or *submission of avails* that in theory will accommodate the needs of the advertiser. This plan includes expected ratings, often

referred to as *projected ratings*, and commercial pricing for each recommended program or daypart. The relationship between audience ratings and pricing is typically expressed as the cost-per-thousand (CPM) households or cost-per-household rating point (CPP). Often an advertiser will ask for additional unit pricing information based on a particular demographic category, such as women ages 18 to 34. Again, more details on these calculations can be found in an upcoming chapter addressing media research.

Before this plan is presented to the client, the sales department wrestles with the complexities of pricing and inventory control. The ultimate goal is to get a maximum price for a limited and perishable inventory without driving business away.

3   The broadcaster and potential buyer negotiate a final plan. For some situations, such as the network "upfront" season, these deals are consummated months in advance of actual airdates.

4   After all the scheduled commercials have been aired, the audience promised is compared to the audience delivered, and appropriate make-goods are implemented if necessary. Finally, the advertiser is billed for services rendered by the broadcaster.

Factors Influencing Pricing

From a television station or network perspective, the following factors influence commercial pricing.

1   *Overall advertiser demand for the medium.* Often a media outlet perceives competition coming from other advertising media. For example, television stations invest much time and energy in attempting to persuade retailers to shift budget dollars away from newspaper advertising. Similarly, radio and cable perceive television as a prime competitor, and so on. Within this context, pricing can be an important factor in diverting budget dollars to different media. A disappointing economy often forces media of all types to compete ruthlessly for dwindling advertising budgets. Historically, certain media have been able to charge higher rates for the same size audience delivered by other media. For instance, broadcast television usually can command higher commercial rates than cable for the same audience delivery.

2   *Specific advertiser demand for target audiences.* It is no secret that some audiences are more attractive to major advertisers than other audiences. Certain age and sex demographics, such as the much-coveted 18–34 young adult, can command a higher cost-per-thousand (CPM) than, say, an older skewing audience. From newspapers and mag-

azines to television and radio, advertiser demand for specific audiences can often influence the content of a media product.

3   *Audience delivery.* Closely related to the desirability of certain audiences is the capacity of the broadcaster to deliver these people in the form of Nielsen program ratings. Consequently, commercial unit pricing can vary greatly across program segments. As discussed earlier, broadcasters often are compelled to forecast ratings performance into the future and then provide make-goods for insufficient audience delivery.

One aspect of the broadcast pricing model that is fairly unique to this particular industry is that certain times of the day are in greater demand than others, regardless of the size of the audience. For instance, a program delivering a 10 rating at 7:00 PM may command a higher unit price than another program airing at 7:00 AM but delivering the same 10 rating. This pricing oscillation would be akin to a gas station changing its per-gallon price every few hours over the course of a typical day. Similarly, for a network or station, the cost-per-thousand pricing parameters can vary from daypart to daypart.

4   *Discounted pricing for large contracts.* Advertisers committing huge budgets to a station or network will receive certain unit pricing discounts. Certainly, this practice can be found in all kinds of business transactions, not just broadcasting. Smaller advertisers suffer the disadvantages of not earning discounted pricing.

5   *Competitor pricing.* The pricing strategies of one's closest competitors can never be ignored. In a highly competitive marketplace, where one media product is considered by an advertiser to be essentially the same as another, stations and networks become suckered into mutually destructive pricing wars, where the only victor is the media buyer who ruthlessly drives down unit pricing.

6   *Intangibles beyond pricing.* Recall that in chapter 3, which dealt with attracting audiences, we focused on the notion of *branding*, the practice of making a media product truly unique. Many brand management principles can be applied to differentiating media brands for advertisers so that a potential buyer may be willing to pay a premium price for a commercial because the program delivers something more than ratings points. For instance, some prime-time programs acquire almost a cult status in which conventional commercial pricing formulas go out the window. *Seinfeld*, discussed earlier, is an example of a program that reached this cult status, commanding extraordinary commercial rates. In more recent times, *Desperate Housewives* has attained the same level of almost-irrational demand by advertisers.

Factors Influencing Inventory Management

From a station perspective, the following are factors influencing control of commercial inventory.

1   *Program commercial format* (local, syndicated, or network). Syndicated and network programs have a prescribed break structure that cannot be altered. For example, the number of local commercial opportunities available in most network programs, particularly in prime time, is considerably less than the number found in local or syndicated programming. Ironically, these few opportunities in prime time are situated within programming that typically delivers a station's highest ratings. The formatting of some local programming, particularly local newscasts, can be adjusted within certain limits, but excessive commercial "clutter" can drive away both audiences and advertisers.

2   *Barter syndication avails.* These avails are the exclusive property of the program syndicator and are sold to national advertisers. Depending on the contractual licensing agreement between the station and the syndicator, the number of these non-revenue-producing barter avails can typically range from 10 to 50 percent of all avails within a program. While barter may reduce the cash outlay for owning a program, it also reduces the number of selling opportunities.

3   *Guaranteed promotion avails.* Recognizing the value of their own air for promoting program content and community image, most stations reserve a specified number of guaranteed or "fixed" promo avails that cannot be used by the sales department.

4   *Make-goods.* As discussed earlier, these "no-charge" commercials are offered to advertisers when originally scheduled commercials are preempted or promised ratings delivery is not achieved.

5   *Product separation and break position guidelines.* Using a computerized coding system, most stations offer a specific amount of brand separation within a product category. For example, a station will not schedule two competing retail furniture store commercials back-to-back within the same break. In addition, many broadcasters offer clients a rotation of insertion positions within breaks or "pods" (the theory being that the first position is most valuable). Determining what break and the position within a break a commercial will be inserted can be a complex task. The area within a station where these scheduling decisions are made every day is called, appropriately, the *traffic department.*

6   *Length of commercial.* Obviously a sixty-second commercial will occupy an avail "space" that could accommodate two thirty-second commercials. Conversely, two fifteen-second announcements can supplant one thirty-second spot. The proper scheduling of

commercials is a daunting task, requiring not only conscientious workers at a station or network but also some sophisticated computer software.[10]

The aforementioned inventory and pricing factors are not mutually exclusive in that unit pricing is adjusted continually in response to the degree of inventory sellout. Logically, as a program's airdate approaches and limited inventory becomes scarcer, unit pricing will typically rise. The opposite trend is also true, in which if demand for inventory remains low as the air date moves closer, unit prices typically fall. Unsold avails are given over to promos and public service announcements.

Preemptions

Many stations' sales departments apply a preemption system to commercial rates by which an avail is essentially put up for auction to the highest bidder, although the station decides on the pricing increments. For example, a commercial inside a popular program may be given three different rates. The top rate of $500 would be designated as "guaranteed" or "non-preemptable." The second rate of $400 would be "preemptable," meaning that if another advertiser is willing to pay the higher price forty-eight hours before air date, this current client's commercial will be preempted or "bumped." A third rate might be $300 and designated as "immediately preemptable," meaning that at any time, without prior notice, the commercial may be preempted. Of course, the station or network has an obligation to reschedule a preempted commercial. The term *preemption* is often confusing to students of broadcasting because the word also refers to the preemption of *network programming* by a station affiliate, meaning the station has decided not to broadcast a specific program in favor of airing something produced locally or acquired through syndication.

'Tis the Season

Regardless of the audience performance of a television station or network, the demand for commercial time by advertisers is highly seasonal. For example, advertising demand is far greater during the fourth quarter of the year (October, November, and December) than the first quarter (January, February, and March). During "slow" weeks, broadcasters will typically introduce incentives, such as discounted rates and special promotions, to fight sluggish sales. One of the prime frustrations for television executives is the statistical fact that the overall highest levels of television (and cable) viewing often occur during the lowest advertiser demand weeks of the year. For instance, the Christmas holiday season leading through New Year's Day usually exhibits extraordinarily high television ratings, but, conversely, retail advertisers for the most part stop their heavy advertising campaigns a week or so before Christmas. The rationale for the abrupt cutback in advertising is not based on viewing habits but on buying habits. January and February are traditionally slow retail months, because most consumers are heavily in debt after the holidays, especially after buying that digital wide-screen television set! Despite strong television viewership, most networks and stations are forced to lower their commercial rates for a while.

Media buying patterns for advertisers can be broken down into roughly three calendar-sensitive markets—*upfront, scatter,* and *opportunistic.* Although the exact terminology is more commonly used by networks and national advertisers, the basic concepts are valid as well for local station operations.

The Upfront Market

The upfront market occurs in early summer when the major networks announce their new fall program schedules. Major advertisers are invited to extravagant parties where they are subjected to all sorts of irrational exuberance and statistical hyperbole about the future of each network. After all this ballyhoo, the real work begins, in which buyers and sellers hammer out long-term agreements based on projected ratings performance. Some major advertisers, such as car manufacturers, will commit as much as 70 percent of their annual advertising budget during the upfront market negotiations. Of course, these contractual agreements allow the advertiser to make ongoing adjustments to this master plan.

The primary advantages for advertisers in making such huge commitments so early in the television season are (a) pricing, (b) fixed placement, and (c) ratings guarantees (through make-goods). When an advertiser in one negotiation purchases literally hundreds of commercials in dozens of programs for many months, the deal becomes an integrated *package,* in which individual unit pricing becomes less stringent. The result is cost effectiveness, just as the total cost of buying a box of a dozen donuts will normally cost less than buying twelve donuts individually. In addition, these commercial rates will not increase even if the program is an unexpected hit. Fixed placement means that the advertiser is assured that a particularly popular, high-demand program will not be sold out when the advertiser, months into the future, wishes to place a commercial. Guaranteed ratings imply that the broadcaster will live up to his or her promised (or "projected") audience delivery. In the event of a shortfall, the broadcaster must provide satisfactory make-good commercials. The annual upfront activity is primarily a network phenomenon. Local television stations tend to be more involved in what has been coined the "scatter market."

The Scatter Market

Advertising budget dollars not committed during the upfront market are set aside for the scatter market, which is divided into four quarters. Although the upfront market offers several advantages, many advertisers find that they cannot anticipate business conditions so many months in advance. Instead, they prefer to dispense their advertising budgets more methodically over the course of the entire year. Networks and stations withhold a limited amount of commercial inventory, anticipating the inevitable scatter market. For an advertiser in a volatile business, this approach may offer more strategic flexibility, but it also comes with the disadvantage of limited choice and the possibility of higher rates. For example, the number of *scatter avails* assigned to a prime-time hit may be so few and in such demand that the estimated unit price may be double or triple the rate paid months earlier by an upfront advertiser. Taking the role of devil's advocate, one might also argue that waiting for some shows to underperform will force pricing down, providing some bargains for the scatter media shopper.

In recent years, advertisers and media buyers have been openly critical of the upfront way of doing business. Many believe that it has outlived its usefulness in that today the emphasis on the traditional fall "Premiere Season" has been displaced by the introduction of many new programs during winter and summer months. Furthermore, business conditions in general seem to be less stable and predictable than in past decades, thereby encouraging companies to place advertising campaigns on much shorter notice. In other words, for many businesses the scatter market style of media buying may be the strategy of choice in coming years. The television industry's response to these criticisms has been rather cordial. From its perspective, a healthy scatter market has the potential of driving sales revenue beyond the "bulk rate" upfront market. In fact, some industry observers predict a transaction environment similar to the hyperactive commodities market, in which items are bought and sold daily, similar to what in broadcasting is known as the opportunistic market.

The Opportunistic Market

As its name implies, the opportunistic market does not involve a great deal of forethought. Instead, it consists of last-minute purchases that could not be anticipated months in advance. As the late John Lennon of the Beatles once said, "Life is what happened while you were busy making other plans," and indeed the opportunistic television commercial market deals with the unexpected. An advertising client suddenly needs additional avails for a newly conceived marketing effort that was not even in the planning stage six months ago. A current advertiser suddenly must cancel a number of scheduled commercials because of a government investigation. A network abruptly cancels a prime-time program, and its new replacement, with a wide-open commercial inventory, must be sold to advertisers right away. There can be any number of business situations where unexpected opportunities emerge for both the buyers and sellers of media.

Sales Partnerships

Since the late 1990s, sales partnerships—in which two or more media outlets join forces to sell commercials in various combination packages— have blossomed. For example, NBC and Telemundo O&O (owned-and-operated) stations, both owned by the same parent, NBC-Universal, share many facilities, including studios, news departments, and sales resources. Sales account executives from either station can approach local advertisers with combination deals. Similarly, CBS and UPN O&O stations now share common corporate parents and therefore offer combination sales packages to local advertisers. Partnering is also evident on a network level, where commonly owned broadcast and cable networks work in tandem to attract major national advertisers. Probably the most obvious business alliance is that of ABC Sports and ESPN, but other less conspicuous sales partnerships still earn handsome profits, such as the relationship between NBC and Bravo.

Program *repurposing* is a natural partnership for a sales strategy in which the advertisers for a *packaged price* can purchase commercial exposures in both broadcast and cable environments. Local station *duopolies* offer similar opportunities for sales partnerships.

Sales Promotion

Promotion strategies aimed at audiences can be quite different from promotion strategies aimed at advertisers, because they do not share the same objectives. For example, a broadcast network might place an ad in

TV Guide with the goal of persuading audiences to tune in to a new prime-time program. The same network might also place an ad in *Advertising Age* with the goal of persuading national advertisers and media buyers to purchase commercials within the program. Consequently, the persuasion tactics and creative components can be radically different. For example, the *TV Guide* ad might address program content and stars, while the *Advertising Age* ad might address the program's Nielsen ratings and unique audience demographics. Station and network sales departments often invest heavily in client parties, presentations, brochures, and other sales paraphernalia, all designed to help advertisers spend their money.

The Television Business Model Under Attack

Earlier we asserted that the business of broadcasting is the *selling of audiences to advertisers*, but in recent years advertisers have begun to question some of the underlying assumptions of this model, the most crucial one being that audiences are actually *exposed* to the commercial message embedded within programming. Whether an exposed audience member is sufficiently persuaded to take action is another matter. In other words, the media are responsible for exposing the message to a target audience, but the media is not responsible if the commercial message is poorly composed. Within this model, audiences are presumed to be available and pay attention to some degree to the commercial. Recent changes in industry practices and audience behavior have some experts predicting "an end to advertising as we know it."[11]

Considerable research from both the private sector and academia has examined the negative effects of two growing problems threatening the television business model. These intertwined factors are (a) the significant increase in commercial "clutter" and (b) the corresponding degree of commercial "zapping" brought on by the introduction of electronic devices such as TiVo. In fact, one could argue that clutter encourages zapping. The bottom line is that audiences may not be paying attention to commercials like they used to.[12]

"Clutter" refers to the excessive number of program interruptions and number of commercials and other non-program material, such as promos, inserted within television programming. The first issue concerning advertisers is the potential loss in commercial effectiveness on audiences. For example, many stations and networks today charge a premium rate to have a commercial inserted at the very first or last position of a break. This "book-ending" strategy assumes the commercials inserted in the middle positions of the break may not be as effective. (So far, research on this is inconclusive.) Despite increasing complaints from advertisers and media planners, television networks and stations have continued to add more commercials. Until advertisers unite and actually refuse to place commercials in overloaded programming, broadcasters will abide by the simple yet powerful precepts of supply and demand. By the way, commercial clutter in general has been determined to be far worse on cable than broadcast television.

A second and more insidious problem is commercial zapping, in which the audience members deliberately avoid exposure to commercials by changing channels. In recent years this has been made easier by the introduction of electronic PVR devices that allow the viewer to record and subsequently play back a program, having edited out unwanted commercials and promos.

Zapping has led to the development of a new type of advertising technique called *product placement* or *product integration*. Here, audiences don't turn away, because the "commercial" is included within the program content itself, similar to the early days of radio, before "spot" commercials became popular. Today this type of advertising is popular particularly with reality programs, in which various props exhibit conspicuous brand logos. Whether the suggestion that participants actually use the branded prop can be as persuasive as a conventional commercial is a question in need of serious research. Some media observers see some thorny ethical issues with product placement in that they believe audiences should be notified somehow of these subtle marketing efforts. The creative community has also expressed concern over this blurring of boundaries between program content and "commercial" insertions in that advertisers are beginning to exert their influence on writers, producers, and directors during the preliminary stages of program scripting and production. Recall that during the early days of radio, sponsors often owned the program outright and merely purchased the air time from broadcasters.

Back to Basics

Sometimes, when we attempt to understand a complex subject, we suffer from an inability to separate "the forest from the trees." Amid all the interacting and changing components of the television business model, there are only three basic strategies for making more money.

1 Sell more product
2 Raise the price
3 Lower the cost of production

These factors often interact with each other. For television broadcasters, the "product" is audiences bundled into commercial breaks and avails. As discussed earlier, increasing the commercial inventory of a program has its limits; nobody will watch a solid hour of nothing but commercials. Unlike for many retail businesses and some print media, the strategy of selling based on volume or limitless inventory does not work well for broadcasters. Given this limitation, the only other practical means of "selling more product" is to have each commercial avail within the fixed inventory deliver bigger audiences and higher ratings. In theory, an advertiser will pay more for a commercial airing inside a program attracting an audience of ten thousand people than one that attracts only one thousand people. Whether the advertiser will pay ten times as much is uncertain, but, in general, bigger audiences foster higher pricing, which is our next strategy.

As noted earlier, pricing is influenced by several factors in addition to the size of a program's audience, such as the health of the economy, the season, competitive pricing maneuvers, and branding. But all these factors share the common denominator of *supply and demand*. For whatever marketing reasons, if an advertiser desperately wants to place a commercial within a specific program of which the inventory is scarce, the price will go up. Just as the price of resort hotel rooms vacillates dramatically according to seasonal tourist demand, so the pricing of television commercials vacillates according to seasonal advertiser demand. Given the fact that a television program's commercial inventory is indeed limited, a shrewd broadcaster can transform this supposed handicap into a "seller's market," in which the scarcity of commercial inventory often drives up commercial rates.

Finally, media managers should also seek ways to enhance earnings by cutting costs. Corporate earnings statements and subsequent stock values don't discriminate between sales and savings. All that matters is bottom-line earnings, and often the most dramatic means of making more money for a business is to reduce the cost of doing business. Check the financial headlines the day after a company discloses massive layoffs, and you will inevitably see the company's stock increase in value. For broadcasters, cutting costs can range from reducing the number of employees by installing automated equipment to rejecting syndicated renewal contracts and opting for less-expensive programming. Of course, the primary way to generate earnings will be through selling audiences to advertisers.

The Case against the Niche

The decades-old assumptions surrounding mass communication have fragmented into the far more complex world of satisfying esoteric needs of audiences. As the number of media competitors has increased dramatically, the old, homogenous "mass audience" is becoming divided and subdivided into an ever-changing array of new demographic and psychographic *niche* categories. A fundamental problem is that, while niche programming may be attractive to audiences and advertisers, the notion of *niche* typically implies *small*, and small is seldom an advantage in any business, including television. In order to survive and prosper, size matters.

Within the field of consumer behavior research, the notion of big brands having disproportionate advantages over small brands is not new. From the financial advantages of economies of scale in reducing costs to the benefits of cultivating customer loyalty, bigger is usually better. As competition becomes more intense due to the increasing number of players, a kind of natural selection occurs that favors the larger, more efficient organizations. Comparing television with cable revenue as an example, we can readily see that, despite all of the doomsday rhetoric aimed at the broadcast television networks, they still manage to control almost half of all television viewing and more than half of all advertising dollars spent on television and cable in the United States. While the portion of the revenue pie designated for conventional broadcasters consists of only a small handful of networks, the designated portion for cable consists of literally hundreds of program networks. Today there is no denying that conventional television broadcasting has lost substantial audiences to cable, but at the same time television broadcasting remains the only way to reach large audiences quickly and efficiently.

In most cases, no single cable network can come close to the prime-time audience delivery of one of the major television networks. True, the glory days of a three- or four-network oligopoly are gone, but conventional broadcast television remains nonetheless a powerful force. Perhaps the most persuasive evidence of the continued financial well-being of television today is the bottom line. Much to the anguish of the cable industry, broadcast television, despite dramatic and ongoing losses in audience ratings, has continued to raise commercial rates year after year.

From a purely economic perspective, we can speculate that excessive niche programming leads to a point of diminishing returns, in which audiences become so tiny that commercial revenue derived from "targeted" advertising cannot offset the cost of doing business. Many production and distribution costs are fixed, regardless of the size of the audience reached. How high a premium price will advertisers pay to reach a small, specialized audience? Judging by the staggering commercial rates that national advertisers are still willing to pay to have their messages seen in network prime-time programs and sporting events, niche marketing has its limits. Even on a local level, most television stations continue to reveal handsome profit margins derived from advertisers who want to place commercials in broad-based programming such as *Oprah, Dr. Phil, Entertainment Tonight, Jeopardy*, and—most important—local newscasts. In years to come, the burning question for television broadcasters will be how to continue to attract and sell *big audiences*.

 ## Questions and Exercises

1   Create a list of the advantages and disadvantages of using television for advertising. What can television do better than other media (such as newspapers, magazines, billboards, radio, the Internet) and vice versa?

2   How much do you agree or disagree with the prediction among some pessimistic industry observers that the long-standing *advertising-based business model* for television is seriously threatened?

3   From an audience perspective, what is you opinion about the ethics of *product placement?*

4   Do you think if television broadcasters reduced the amount of *commercial clutter* contained within programs, viewers would zap commercials less often? Explain your opinion.

5   Pretend that you and a friend have set up a lemonade stand in front of your house, and a week later your next-door neighbor decides to set up another stand. Taking a *systems approach*, describe all the interdependent factors that you and your friend need to consider when establishing the best price for a glass of lemonade?

Playing by the Rules

Regulating the Business of Television

Now that we have examined the interwoven components of technology and economics, a third factor to introduce to our system is regulation. We need to be careful with definitions, because "regulation" can be understood in several ways. First, from a purely economic standpoint, the term often is used in the context of the "natural" regulating forces of a free marketplace. Another variation of the term has been self-regulation, depicting the controlling influence of nongovernmental industry organizations that impose ethical standards of conduct on their members. Finally, formalized law and policy guidelines for the industry can be called government regulation. This chapter will address all three, but the primary emphasis will be on government regulation and, in particular, the FCC.

Free-Market "Regulation"

Advocates of the free enterprise business model assume that the marketplace "regulates" itself through the age-old forces of supply and demand, the underlying theory being that through unfettered competition, good products and services inevitably force out bad products and services, resulting in ever-increasing benefits for consumers. Of course, this brief definition is overly simplistic, but it is important to appreciate the fact that, historically, the American culture has leaned toward a free and open market for solving problems, coupled with a certain distrust of government. This may not appear all that obvious in light of the many government agencies that now exist, but compared to the rest of the world, American government remains one of the least intrusive.

Today, with the introduction of digital technology that can provide almost limitless opportunities for electronic expression through cable, satellite, and the Internet, many industry leaders and legal scholars assert that the over-the-air broadcast spectrum is no longer a scarce public resource and that government meddling is therefore unnecessary. This posture has its origins in the 1980s under the Reagan Administration, when FCC chair Mark Fowler became an outspoken critic of media regulation. This was somewhat surprising in that a major government insider was advocating less government. Fowler and his supporters disagreed with many of the underlying assumptions of the original Communication Act of 1934, including the notion of public ownership of the airwaves and government approval to buy and sell stations. Additionally, Fowler was annoyed that at that time the FCC was flirting with content regulation, requiring stations to assign annual quotas for news, public affairs, and educational programming. Fowler's opinions were heavily on the side of business:

> Communications policy should be directed toward maximizing the services the public desires. Instead of defining public demand and specifying categories of programming to serve this demand, the Commission should rely on the broadcasters' ability to determine the wants of their audiences through the normal mechanisms of the marketplace.[1]

This school of thought assumes that the invisible hand of the marketplace will automatically produce desirable results. Neither Congress nor the majority of Fowler's fellow commissioners entirely embraced this marketplace approach, but in subsequent years this notion of deregulation gradually became more popular. The 1996 Telecommunications Act was considered a major breakthrough in putting the brakes on government intervention in station ownership limitations, license renewal standards, and restrictions on cable and telephone companies entering each other's business domains. A decade later, as this book is being written, the FCC, under pressure from a number of court decisions questioning the wisdom of media regulation, is attempting to further deregulate television. The most important areas from a business perspective deal with restrictions on the number of stations a company can own and barriers to owning or partnering with other media, such as newspapers and cable systems. According to the courts, the FCC must justify regulation with persuasive empirical evidence that the free market is better served with certain legal restrictions in place.

This emphasis on free enterprise coincides with the uniquely American notion of free expression. Few countries in the world, including most industrialized democracies, have a written statute as elegant and powerful as the First Amendment to the Constitution. Throughout American history, the regulation of media in general has been influenced greatly by the First Amendment.

> Congress shall make no law respecting an establishment of religion, or prohibiting the free exercise thereof; or abridging the freedom of speech, or of the press; or the right of the people peaceably to assemble, and to petition the Government for a redress of grievances.[2]

This brief statement has been the underlying philosophical touchstone for many important court decisions denying government regulation. That is, in order for the government to intervene in the business of media, particularly in the area of regulating content, truly compelling reasons must be found. Research indicates that while most people believe in the overall principle of free speech, they also believe in certain restrictions, as have the courts. Issues of national security, inciting to riot, defamation of character, and pornography are just some of the court-imposed restrictions on free speech. Some people want greater restrictions on media content, but the Supreme Court in dozens of cases usually has sided with the advocates of "the marketplace of ideas" in which a free society must tolerate offensive expression in order to guarantee healthy public discourse.

The philosophical convergence of free enterprise and free speech can be seen in an often-quoted statement made by Supreme Court Justice Oliver Wendell Holmes in 1919: "The ultimate good desired is better reached by free trade in ideas, and the test of truth is the power of the thought to get itself accepted in the competition of the market."[3]

Furthermore, the high court has been especially lenient with news media, recognizing the possible chilling effect on good investigative journalism if reporters fear government reprisals. In defamation cases, even when incompetence or negligence can be found on the part of a reporter, the court will not condone prosecution unless the accuser can prove actual malice, which is defined as "knowledge of falsity or a reckless disregard for the truth."[4] The underlying message here is that journalists are allowed to make mistakes.

Public figures, in particular politicians and government officials, receive less protection than ordinary citizens in terms of libel and invasion of privacy. The courts consistently have ruled that some people deliberately thrust themselves into the public spotlight, among them professional athletes, entertainers, and politicians, and therefore these public figures should expect a certain level of commentary and criticism that is "newsworthy." On the other hand, an ordinary citizen not seeking publicity should be entitled in some situations to challenge the First Amendment protection given to the press.

One area of particular concern to media and advertisers is a special type of expression called commercial speech. As the name implies, this includes advertisements for products and services. Unlike political speech, which is given almost total constitutional protection, or obscene speech, which is given no protection whatsoever, commercial speech falls somewhere in the middle. After all, the primary purpose of a commercial or an ad is not to express creativity but to move product. As a result, the Supreme Court does not see commercial speech as deserving of the same constitutional protection afforded to a newscast, a political debate, or a work of art. The regulatory posture is quite paternalistic in that the court assumes that people are somewhat gullible and do not always use proper judgment. Providing information about lawful products and services is clearly entitled to constitutional protection, but false or deceptive selling strategies are not tolerated. For risky products such as alcohol, gambling, or drugs, the courts have been particularly tough. Given this judicial First Amendment framework, government agencies such as the Federal Trade Commission and the Food and Drug Administration keep a close eye on commercial speech.

Self-Regulation

Admitting that a completely unfettered marketplace may be too much freedom, most major American industries have established organizations that provide ethical guidelines or codes for business behavior. Individual companies typically become subscribing members of the organization and participate in its governance. Although violations of the member guidelines and ethical codes typically do not result in fines and certainly not in jail time, they can result in embarrassing sanctions, unwanted negative publicity, and possible ostracism. Self-regulation has been used by many industries as a preemptive strategy to halt formalized government regulation. The working theory is that if these market-driven businesses can effectively police themselves, there is no need to invite government intercession. An example would be the Radio and Television News Director Association (RTNDA), which has established a comprehensive code of ethics for working journalists.[5]

Many of these organizations, such as the National Association of Broadcasters (NAB),[6] also serve as government lobbying groups whose goal is not necessarily the halting of proposed government rule-making but rather the passage of statutes and bills that may assist the business goals of the industry. Some critics see a kind of double standard among these organizations in that on one hand they advocate a competitive free market and self-regulation, but on the other hand, when the same free market appears to threaten the prosperity of a specific business, the organization (sometimes called a "trade group") turns to government agencies or Congress for protection. An example is the ongoing controversy between television broadcasters and the cable industry over digital multicasting. When the cable industry, represented by the National Cable and Telecommunications Association (NCTA),[7] formally refused to automatically retransmit all digital sub-channels utilized by a television station, insisting that stations should compete for carriage just like any other cable content provider, the NAB ran howling to the FCC for government intervention. So far, the FCC has not intervened, essentially siding with the cable position.

Although the broad definition of the term ethics deals with "what is good and bad and with moral duty and obligation"[8] in the contemporary world of business, the word "ethics" is often used to mean behavior that is unacceptable but not necessarily illegal. Most codes of ethics for media organizations address issues that would not be considered a violation of the law. For example, a newscast showing a close-up of a dead soldier's face may be considered unethical but is not a genuine crime. Media ethics in this context is a constant topic of discussion and debate among audiences and professionals.[9] Our next section looks at media regulations that, if violated, have serious consequences.

Government Regulation

A counter argument to the free-market approach assumes that because private markets are dedicated to satisfying personal desires rather than public values, there is no reason to assume that the market, if left to its own devices, will produce an appropriate level of needed information and discourse. Furthermore, self-regulation is more often a sham than a serious tool for promoting ethical behavior. Rather than defining the public interest as what the public wants, the definition should be what the public needs. According to this regulatory approach, a preoccupation with popularity and profits is not necessarily in the best interests of a democracy. From the perspective of television, this argument is not new.

Decades ago, legendary broadcast journalist Edward R. Morrow lamented,

> If we were to do the Second Coming of Christ for a full hour, there would
> be a considerable number of stations which would decline to carry it on the
> grounds that a western or a quiz show would be more profitable.[10]

A less draconian approach to the industry-regulation relationship is to use government only when the marketplace appears not to be self-correcting or the industry participants fail at self-regulation. Under these circumstances, the government is compelled to step in and solve the problem. The identification of genuine problems and the determination of the best solutions are often hotly debated within government agencies and the halls of Congress. In particular, the broadcasting industry has been singled out as unique from other types of media and, therefore, deserving of extraordinary government oversight and less First Amendment protection.

Broadcasting Is Unique among Media

Suppose you wanted to start your own newspaper. Must a newspaper owner request a government license to publish? Before starting the presses, must a newspaper owner prove to the government financial solvency, technical expertise, and good character? Must a newspaper owner ask approval from the government to purchase more newspapers? Must a newspaper owner by law provide special discount advertising rates for political candidates? Must a newspaper owner be held liable for publishing words or pictures that are deemed by the government to be not obscene but indecent? The correct answer to all of these questions is no, but substitute the word "newspaper" with the words "broadcast station," and the correct answer to the same questions becomes yes.

The core rationale for this extraordinary governmental scrutiny goes back to broadcasting's special technological constraints. As presented in chapter 2, which dealt with television technology, the problems of spectrum scarcity and interference opened the door early on to some type of government regulation in the name of "the public interest, convenience, and necessity." Implied in this rationale, of course, is the suspicion that the free market cannot always regulate itself properly. The oldest argument looks at the supposed chaos in the assignment of radio frequencies to radio stations in the 1920s. Without somebody to set technical standards and enforce operating procedures, the airwaves would be nothing but bedlam. That somebody became the U.S. government. Some historians argue that given sufficient time, these undisciplined broadcasters, out of pure self-interest, would eventually have united to set up a privately supported self-regulatory organization to cure the technological mess.[11]

The Federal Communications Commission was established by the Communications Act of 1934 as a U.S. government agency independent of the executive branch and directly responsible to Congress. The commission regulates television, radio, wire, satellite, and cable in the fifty states and all U.S. territories. There are five commissioners who direct the FCC. They are appointed by the president and confirmed by the Senate. Only three commissioners can be of the same political party at any given time, and none can have a financial interest in any commission-related business. The president selects one of the commissioners to serve as chairperson. All commissioners, including the chairperson, have five-year terms, except when filling an unexpired term.

During the early days of radio, the overarching regulatory attitude was what some legal scholars have coined a "traffic cop" approach in that the goal was primarily to organize efficiently the limited airwaves for the public benefit. This was as far as most industry leaders, politicians, and the public wanted government to become involved in broadcasting. Of course the air waves themselves would be considered public property, but any ideas about the federal government actually managing media outlets (that is, owning and operating stations and networks) was quickly squelched in favor of privately owned, profit-seeking companies. Later, part of the spectrum would be reserved for noncommercial use, but for the most part, the American system of broadcasting from its inception in the 1920s has been understood to be a commercial business. But despite being recognized as a private business, the broadcasting industry has still come under special regulations to safeguard public access and audience sensibilities.

In 1969 the basic authority of the FCC was questioned in a seminal U.S. Supreme Court case entitled *Red Lion Broadcasting v. FCC*, which asserted, among other things, that the physical limitations in the broadcast spectrum—both for radio and television—indeed justify government licensing of broadcasters and the allocation of specific frequencies or channels in which to operate. Given this technological premise, the court also condoned a certain amount of content regulation in terms of assuring access to the airwaves by the public to express contrary opinions (in particular a rule called the Fairness Doctrine, which has since been revoked). The high court asserted that "the First Amendment provides no sanctuary for unlimited private censorship operating a medium not open to all."[12]

In addition to resolving technical challenges, advocates of government regulation have maintained over the years that broadcasting is unique because of its pervasiveness. That is, radio and television program content is so pervasive that it tends to intrude on a captive audience that cannot easily turn away. Unlike consumers of other types of media, such as books, newspapers, and magazines, broadcast audiences are more vulnerable to being unexpectedly exposed to offensive content. The Supreme Court has not only supported this notion about free over-the-air television but has allowed cable and satellite programming to escape from these restrictions because it is a subscriber-based business and, therefore, customers supposedly have a heightened awareness of what they are purchasing. The assumption being that exposure to cable and satellite content is more deliberate than accidental. Consequently, most issues dealing with offensive media content, such as indecency, have been strictly the problem of broadcasters.

Now that we have examined why broadcasting has always been considered a unique medium, deserving of more government regulation than other media, we will focus on some of the important functions of the FCC. Aside from the need for a "traffic cop," radio and television broadcasting has fostered additional regulation addressing issues of (a) permission to use the airwaves through licensing, (b) limitations on station ownership and cross-ownership with other media, and (c) rules regarding program content.

Licensing

The FCC is granted the authority to issue and renew station licenses for the operation of all radio and television stations in the United States This licensing process does not include networks, although most networks do own several stations. These network-owned-and-operated stations (O&Os) are subject to the same FCC regulations as all other stations.

A licensee must satisfy several criteria, including being a citizen of the United States. If a company seeks a license, it must have no more than 25 percent foreign ownership. The individual or company also must demonstrate sufficient funding to operate the station for at least three months with no other earned revenue coming in, and the applicant must be of good character, which usually means the person or company has stayed out of serious legal trouble. Another stipulation, though modified in recent years, is that the proposed licensee complies with FCC ownership limits. That is, the government can restrict the total number of stations an individual or company can own nationwide and within an individual market.

For the licensing renewal process, the commission is charged with the duty of determining whether the station has operated in the public interest during its licensing period, which is currently eight years. Rarely have stations lost their licenses. More often, violations are punished by fines or warnings. The Telecommunications Act of 1996 revised the criteria for challenging license renewals by instituting a two-step process in which, if the incumbent license holder has demonstrated that it has served the public interest adequately and has met all statutory and regulatory requirements, it will be granted a renewal automatically. Only if the broadcaster has not fulfilled these obligations will the FCC initiate the second step of listening to formal challenges from individuals or groups that may promise better performance and wish to take over the license. Again, this is extremely rare, but nevertheless, the guiding principle that broadcast stations, unlike other media, must be licensed by the government, is still a part of the broadcasting industry system.

Ownership Restrictions

Given the historical underpinnings of free enterprise and free expression, an important, recurring theme of much regulation of the media in this country has been the encouragement of competition, which in turn has prodded the government to impose ownership limitations. Throughout its history, the FCC has successfully argued that limitations on the number of stations a company can own serve the public interest by encouraging competition, diversity, and innovation. This posture was far more convincing when the television spectrum was indeed a scarce public resource with only a handful of channels available to each community and program content dominated by the Big Three networks of NBC, CBS, and ABC. With the expansion of cable in the 1980s and later the development of new media technologies such as direct-to-home satellite transmission and, of course, the Internet, using the scarcity principle to justify media ownership restrictions has lost much of its legal and philosophical punch. Over the years the FCC has altered several times the number of radio and television stations a single company or organization could legally own. For instance, in 1985 the ownership limit was increased from seven to twelve stations. The Telecommunications Act of 1996 changed the unit of measure by abandoning the notion of the mere number of stations and adopting instead a new metric that looks at the total population coverage achieved by a group of stations. Using census data and signal coverage maps, the FCC can estimate the total number of households a station potentially reaches. The combined market populations for all stations owned by one company are then converted into a simple percentage of the total U.S. population. Initially the commission set a threshold of 25 percent. This was subsequently increased to 35 percent and then 39 percent.

The 1996 act requires the FCC to examine its media ownership rules every two years, and, in 2003, the FCC revised its limits for broadcast ownership after completing an extensive, twenty-month review. This was motivated in part by two federal court decisions striking down some of its existing rules and requiring the FCC to do a better job of justifying any limits on media ownership now that media competition appears unencumbered—thanks to new, multi-channel media technologies. A special task force was charged with developing a solid factual foundation for re-evaluating FCC media ownership policies that promote competition, diversity, and localism in today's media market.

The final recommendations were controversial, to say the least, essentially advocating a massive deregulation of station ownership rules and cross-ownership rules involving newspapers and cable systems. Multiple parties appealed the decisions in various federal appellate courts, and, as of this writing, these appeals are still pending.

Content Regulation

The FCC has dabbled in content regulation over the years. For example, during elections broadcasters must provide "equal opportunity" for all qualified candidates to express their views on relevant issues. Newscasts, public affairs programs, and live coverage of news events are excluded, so the real emphasis is on the purchase of commercials. Although the broadcaster is not compelled to air the same number of commercials for each candidate, the opportunity to buy time must be open to all qualified persons. That is, once the management of a station agrees to accept political advertising, it cannot be selective as to who can have access to the station and who cannot. During election years, political advertising is a huge source of revenue for stations. As a result, the broadcasting industry is not a big advocate of recent campaign finance reform initiatives that might limit television advertising. The NAB sees such regulation as an encroachment on the First Amendment. Another example of content regulation is the Children's Television Act of 1990, which imposes an obligation on television stations to offer educational programming for children. It also mandated that manufacturers of television sets install "v-chips" to coincide with the development of a violence ratings system so that parents could monitor and automatically block violent programs.

The most controversial content regulation in recent years concerns the notion of indecency, in which a station can possibly be fined or even lose its license. Unlike our earlier examples of content scrutiny which addressed the public accessibility to the media, information and ratings about programming, indecency rulings go after the acceptability of the content for airing. While legally obscene content can be prosecuted in all media, including print, indecency is a concept directed exclusively at radio and television. Although both violations deal with sexual activity, obscene programming is prohibited at all times, while the lesser offense of indecent programming is allowed during late evening hours, typically when children are supposed to be in bed. In this sense the commission is not censoring content but rather redirecting it to what it calls "safe harbors" for adult consumption. Indecent content is defined as "patently offensive as measured by contemporary community standards for the broadcast medium and describes sexual or excretory activities and organs." If this material, taken as whole, does not demonstrate a "serious literary, artistic, political or scientific value," it may be deemed obscene and rejected categorically, especially when the sexual activity appeals to the "prurient interest" of an audience. Although defining obscenity in real-world situations has often been controversial, applying a practical definition of indecency has been even more exasperating. The interpretation of indecency has changed over time, depending both on who is appointed chairman of the FCC and the philosophical leanings of the White House. Based on recent FCC decisions, broadcasters seem baffled as to what will get them in trouble and what will not. Consequently, many programming decision-makers have become overly cautious. For example, some news directors are reluctant to do certain on-the-scene, live interviews for fear that the person being interviewed will say something "indecent." For live talk shows, this anxiety has fostered the use of time delays in which a program producer has a few seconds to preview the content and "bleep" suspect language. Critics claim that the commission's lack of clarity has had a chilling effect on creativity and aggressive journalism. Aggravating the situation even more is the fact that none of the examples of content regulation presented here are applicable to cable, satellite, newspapers, magazines, or other media—just radio and television. (In recent years, influential members of Congress have proposed expanding indecency rulings to include cable.)

Content regulation can take the form of file-keeping and surveys in that stations are required to maintain detailed public files, including daily station logs that stipulate the exact air times of all programs and commercials. Additionally, stations are encouraged to record and archive all newscasts for several weeks, with individual stories cataloged and saved for years. On a quarterly basis, stations must also file documents that disclose important community issues and local programs that have addressed these issues, including newscasts.

The Decision-Making Process

The FCC is responsible for developing and modifying broadcasting and other media rules and policies in order to address changing technologies, changing competition and ownership patterns. A detailed explanation of the entire structure and function of the FCC can be found at its website.[13]

When the commission makes a decision to create a new ruling or modify significantly an existing rule, it follows a very methodical process.

- Notice of Inquiry (NOI): The commission releases an NOI to gather information about a broad subject or as a means of generating ideas on a specific issue. The topics can range from technical standards, such as determining the technical specifications for HDTV transmissions, to inquiring about the influence of violent program content on young children. After reviewing comments from the public in response to an NOI, the FCC may issue a Notice of Proposed Rulemaking (NPRM).

- Notice of Proposed Rulemaking (NPRM): An NPRM contains proposed changes to the FCC's rules and seeks public comment on these proposals.

- Further Notice of Proposed Rulemaking (FNPRM): After reviewing comments to the NPRM, the FCC may choose to issue an FNPRM regarding specific issues raised in the comments. The FNPRM provides an opportunity for the public to comment further on a specific or related proposal. After considering comments to an NPRM or FNPRM, the FCC commissioners decide whether the issue warrants legal action in the form of a formal Report and Order.

- Report and Order (R&O): The R&O may develop new rules, amend existing rules, or make a decision not to do so. Summaries of the R&O are published in the Federal Register. Once again, the procedures allow for critical comments by any concerned citizen or organization in the form of a Petition for Reconsideration.

- Petition for Reconsideration: A formal petition must be filed with the commission within thirty days of the date that the R&O appears in the Federal Register. The commission then ponders the validity of the complaints against the R&O and decides whether reconsideration is necessary. Regardless of the outcome of deliberations, the commissioners issue a Memorandum Opinion and Order (MO&O).

- Memorandum Opinion and Order (MO&O): In response to a Petition for Reconsideration, the FCC issues a Memorandum Opinion and Order or an Order on Reconsideration amending the new rules or stating that the rules will not be changed.

- Public Notice (PN): Throughout the above-mentioned procedures, the industry and the public are notified in the form of a Public Notice (PN). A PN is issued to notify the public of an action taken or the scheduling of an upcoming meeting or hearing.

Other Sources of Regulation

Although for most people the FCC is probably the most familiar source of regulation, the federal courts, Congress, and the White House all have influence over the business of broadcasting. Furthermore, these sources seldom operate in isolation, but rather interact with each other. For example, although the White House does not directly regulate broadcasting per se, the president appoints all FCC commissioners, including the chair. This power is moderated by the fact that the U.S. Senate must confirm the president's selections. The executive branch oversees a number of agencies that can have a profound influence on broadcasting. Among these are the Department of Justice, which keeps close tabs on transfers of media ownership and antitrust activity. Because broadcasters make use of an advertising-based business model, the Federal Trade Commission often becomes involved with radio and television operators as distributors of commercials. On a more informal level, the White House can assert considerable influence on the broadcasting industry through "friendly persuasion." The most notable example in recent years has been the broadcast networks' acceptance of a voluntary content ratings system focusing on sex and violence.

Overseeing all of the above-mentioned regulatory players are the federal courts, including the U.S. Court of Appeals and the Supreme Court. In theory, the courts are not supposed to create policy but merely decide whether a particular policy is legal. Most often, the courts deal with FCC rulings in which opposing parties maintain that the commission did not follow established procedures or acted beyond its authority. In some cases, the courts will address media-related rulings made by the House and Senate, such as several congressional attempts to regulate content on the Internet.

Economic versus Social Regulation: Can the Two Be Separated?

Study of the regulatory process has frequently categorized activities as either economic or social in their intent. The rationale for economic regulation has been "market failure," in which free enterprise has generated negative consequences such as media monopolies. The rationale for social regulation tends to be more subjective in that it addresses the "physical, moral or aesthetic wellbeing of the population," such as rules addressing broadcast indecency. The FCC historically has straddled both types of regulation and, in fact, we could argue that these categories often overlap.[14] Returning to our systems approach, we can see how a crossover effect is possible. For example, in order to stimulate business competition (lower prices, more innovation, better service, and so on) in the name of the public interest, the FCC initiates an economic regulation addressing station ownership that ostensibly is non-content regulation. The same concern over concentration of private ownership, however, is intertwined with several important content related issues addressing the free flow of ideas and the availability of divergent viewpoints. That is, lack of competition in a free market is bad not only for business but for democracy. Of course these same worries about the power of Big Business can readily be applied to the power of Big Government. The stifling of the free flow of ideas can also be the result of a paternalistic, overly intrusive government. For decades the real regulatory challenge for the FCC has been to stimulate fair competition without succumbing to the temptations of censorship.

Technology and social philosophy sometimes collide in unexpected ways. A good historical example is the FCC deliberations over the introduction of UHF. Because of the inherent scarcity of spectrum, the commission had to arrive at a formula that would not only solve the technical headaches of interference but also address the more abstract political issues of serving a democracy. The upcoming case study on UHF and the quest for a fourth network (chapter 7) shows how, with the best of intentions, a regulatory decision can result in an unintended calamity. Today the much-publicized technological transition from analog to digital television transmission in the United States may be far more than a simple "nuts and bolts" changeover. Instead, the unintended social consequences of making the analog television set essentially obsolete and coercing citizens to buy new and relatively expensive digital television sets may be as tumultuous as the adoption of UHF.

Controlling Convergence

A growing dilemma for the FCC is media convergence, since broadcasting can no longer be conveniently isolated from other media. A statement made by Barbara Cherry, deputy chief of the Office of Plans and

Policy, resonates with our systems approach to understanding the place of broadcasting within a larger digital landscape.

> Because of the development of digital technology, the telecommunications and mass media industries no longer serve fully separable economic markets. Rather, these industries now provide some substitutable services and uses. The economic interrelationships also create interdependencies among these industries' historically distinct regulatory regimes so that policy change within one regime may have spillover effects for others.[15]

A good example might be the legal entanglements of a licensed television station supporting its own Internet website in which it digitally "streams" programming that originally aired on its conventional over-the-air channel. Is this repurposed Internet content subject to the same regulations as its broadcast version? Would such programming run into problems of indecency in one case but not the other?

Probably the biggest regulatory collision will be the convergence of broadcasting and print media, because for decades they have operated according to two very different regulation models. In the print model, publishers are essentially autonomous, protected against almost all forms of government interference. In the broadcasting model, stations are perceived as trustees of the electronic spectrum, acting in the public interest, convenience, and necessity, and consequently subject to FCC regulation to ensure the stations live up to their obligations. This "hands-off" versus "hands-on" dichotomy between print and broadcasting is fast becoming obsolete in a converged media universe. These and dozens more perplexing "cross-platform" challenges will face the FCC and other regulatory organizations in coming years.

Questions for Further Thought

1   Look up the *Red Lion v. FCC Supreme Court* case and think about the court's arguments for reaffirming the authority of the FCC. Do you believe the arguments are still persuasive?

2   Look up the *NYT v. Sullivan Supreme Court* case and think about the court's arguments for avoiding a "chilling effect" on journalists. Do you agree or disagree with the degree of freedom and forgiveness given news organizations?

3   Provide an example of "The Free Market of Ideas" in which an open and public debate is better for a society than requesting that the government resolve the problem.

4   In your opinion, what is the maximum number of television stations a company should legally own? Explain your answer in terms of (a) economic and (b) social consequences.

5   In addition to the items presented in this chapter, provide more examples of how media convergence will present some difficult regulatory challenges in years to come.

Counting Heads

Television's Obsession
with Research and Ratings

This topic was selected to be a separate chapter because of the enormous influence that ratings and other audience research have on the television industry. In fact, ratings have a role in most of the chapters of this book. From attracting and selling audiences to provoking government regulation and reconciling disputes between networks and stations, the need to measure audience behaviors and attitudes is always in the background. Although the industry supports several types of research, Nielsen ratings are the gold standard.

From a systems perspective we can say confidently that ratings interact in some fashion with all the major components of the commercial television system. For networks and most television stations, these data help determine

- Whether a program will be renewed or cancelled
- How much an advertiser will pay for a commercial
- The need for government regulation
- The overall profitability of the network or station
- The job security and promotion possibilities for all types of media managers

General managers, program directors, sales managers, and even news directors are often preoccupied with these figures. Clients use Nielsen ratings to buy and sell television time as well as to make program decisions. Nielsen rating points have been called the true "currency" in most transactions between buyers and sellers, which adds up to more than $60 billion in national and local advertising spending in the United States each year. Nielsen makes money by selling its data to "subscribers."

Ratings also have a spillover effect on other related businesses. For example, if a program is cancelled, hundreds of creative people—producers, writers, actors, and production personnel—lose their jobs. On the other hand, a cancelled program means an opportunity for a replacement program, which in turn means work in the same job positions.

Ratings also have a societal effect in that only the most popular programs, as measured by Nielsen ratings, remain available to be experienced by the public. In addition, ratings and other audience research are often used in telecommunications policy debates in Congress and at the FCC. Often both sides, in a heated exchange over the need for new regulation, will turn to Nielsen ratings to bolster their arguments. It is no accident that the National Association of Broadcasters retains a substantial research department intended primarily to help support the political agendas of the broadcasting industry.

Since the 1940s, several companies have entered the television audience measurement business, but only Nielsen has survived. For many years the Arbitron Company served as a respectable competitor for local market television ratings, but in 1994 the company withdrew from the fray, deciding to focus exclusively on its more profitable radio ratings service. Since that time, Nielsen Media Research has had a virtual monopoly on television audience measurement in the United States. Broadcasters and advertisers are not thrilled with this arrangement. One trade magazine writer refers to Nielsen as " . . . a creaking giant about to be overwhelmed by new technologies."[1] The core problem is that whenever a new competitor attempts to muscle in on Nielsen's territory, the same critical broadcasters and advertisers have provided only lukewarm support, primarily with rhetoric rather than with revenue.

Recently the Arbitron Company patented a revolutionary electronic device for measuring television audiences and contemplated challenging Nielsen head-on, but as Steve Morris, the company's CEO, confessed:

> There's a long history of people taking runs at the incumbent. But there's no half way here. If we go after Nielsen, it would be war, and at the end of the day there would be one person standing . . . and believe me, there are skeletons littering the trail.[2]

Ultimately Arbitron sought a partnership with Nielsen, but as of the writing of this text, Nielsen has decided rather abruptly to end the marriage.

We begin this chapter with an overview of how ratings research is used within the industry, including some common terminology. The second section explains some of the fundamentals of sample-based research methods and statistical procedures. Finally, we take a close look at Nielsen's methodology and services.

How Ratings Are Used within the Television Industry

Because the basic business model of television is the selling of audiences to advertisers, both the buyers and sellers of these audiences want to know as accurately as possible just how many people are watching any given program. Additionally, they want to know what types of people watch. Typically this information is presented as *demographics*, highlighting characteristics such as age, sex, and place of residence. Unlike newspapers or magazines, in which the media company can count exactly how many copies of a particular publication are sold, there has been no simple way to accomplish this for electronic media, such as radio, television, and cable. Nielsen Media Research estimates audience size and demographic composition by drawing a *random sample* of a designated population, such as a local television market, and infers mathematically that, within certain margins of error, the audience viewing activity found in the sample is similar to that of the larger population.

Broadcast audiences are typically quantified into rating "points," which are bought and sold as a commodity in a competitive marketplace. In essence, each rating point contributes to the overall monetary value of a commercial. Using the analogy of a factory, networks and stations use programming and marketing strategies to "manufacture" rating points. The points are then sold to advertisers. This packaging of audiences fosters a business jargon that sounds very "retail," such as *audience delivery, inventory, sellout levels,* and *cost per thousand*. If we could eavesdrop on a typical negotiation between a station sales representative and a media buyer, we would notice that audiences are seldom referred to as "people." Instead, the conversation would be injected with phrases dealing with "points."

What Nielsen Media Research means by a "television rating" or "rating point" is not the same as the common use of the word "rating," which usually is a subjective attitude or opinion of how much a person liked or appreciated something, such as a movie, restaurant, or a book. On the contrary, "ratings" in television terminology are not measures of attitudes but of behavior. Broadcast ratings for both radio and television do not reflect how much the sample participants liked a given program, just whether they *watched* or not. Of course, we logically can assume that a highly viewed program is also liked.

Ratings are broken down into two fundamental measures—*rating points* and *share points*. Both are percentages, although the word percentage normally is not included in discussions about ratings among professionals.

A program *rating* is the size of an audience expressed as a percentage of the total population of the market under study. For example, in a market consisting of 120,000 households, suppose a program airing at 7:00 PM attracts a total of 30,000 of these households. Converting this to a percentage, 120,000 divided by 30,000 equals a *rating* of 25, or 25 rating points.

A program *share* is the size of an audience expressed as a percentage of the households or people actually watching television at that time. Returning to our earlier example, let us assume that at 7:00 PM, 60,000 households are watching television. This is expressed by Nielsen as Households Using Television, or HUT. Now, instead of comparing our audience of 30,000 households to the total population, we compare this figure to our HUT level. Converting this to a percentage, we divide 60,000 by 30,000, which yields an audience *share* of 50, or 50 share points.

Most formal reports and trade magazine articles examining television program performance present both rating and share data. Often *whole numbers* (for instance, our 30,000 households) are displayed alongside the program rating and share. This allows media professionals to analyze the program from a number of perspectives. In general, sales representatives and media buying personnel tend to look at whole numbers and ratings, while programming and marketing people tend to scrutinize share figures. It is customary within the industry not to include percentage signs (%) next to rating and share data. Furthermore, these measures often are displayed in tandem with a slash mark, such as 25/50, implying a 25 rating and a 50 share.

Nielsen ratings information is not restricted only to households. Age and sex information is converted to whole numbers and ratings points (but not share points). These demographic "cells," such as women ages 18 to 49 or men ages 25 to 54, are used both by broadcasters and advertisers to better understand the audience delivery patterns of different programs. Program executives will often create an *audience profile* for a particular program, comparing several key demographic categories with the total audience delivery. This information is usually expressed as a proportion or percentage of the total audience. For instance, a report might reveal that 30 percent of the persons watching a particular program fall within the 18–34 age bracket, while the remaining 70 percent fall within much older categories. This statistical leaning toward a particular age or sex demographic is often called a program's audience *skew* (for instance,

Monday Night Football "skewed" toward young men). The results from these profile studies allow network and station management people to see the relative audience strengths and weaknesses of their own programming and that of competitors. Armed with such information, program producers may want to manipulate certain elements of a production, such as characters or storylines, to enhance a key demographic segment that appears deficient. Whether such a deficiency is truly important is a function of advertiser demand, which brings us to our next topic of how ratings are used in the buying and selling of audiences.

Given this ratings information, the cost of a commercial is often evaluated in terms of unit pricing. Just as you evaluate the cost efficiency of a gallon of gas for your car by looking at the posted per-gallon price, so media buyers examine the unit pricing of key audience categories. The most common expressions are *cost-per-thousand* or CPM (M is the Roman numeral for thousand) and *cost-per-point* or CPP. Let's go back to our earlier example to clarify these procedures.

Now suppose a station wants to sell a commercial for $600 within this program. A savvy media buyer will look at this offer from a *unit cost* perspective. Starting with households, the buyer may want to calculate the *cost-per-thousand* (CPM) households. The math is fairly simple; first determine the number of 1,000s the program delivers, which in this case would be 30 (that is, 30,000 households divided by 1,000). Then calculate the cost-per-thousand by dividing the total commercial cost of $600 by 30, yielding a unit cost CPM of $20. An alternative procedure would be to focus on household rating points and come up with a *cost-per-household rating point* (CPP). In our example, recall that the program generated a 25 rating. Dividing the total commercial cost of $600 by 25 yields a CPP of $24. Unit costs for various demographic categories can be calculated using the identical CPM and CPP unit cost procedures.

Suppose our program delivers 1,000 women ages 18–34. Let's also assume that a total of 20,000 women ages 18–34 live in the market. This means that the program generates a *5 rating* (or 5 "demo rating") for that particular target demographic (20,000 divided by 1,000).

These calculations are not as absolute as they might appear. Recall that most networks and stations sell commercial time weeks or even months ahead of scheduled air dates. Therefore, ratings performance is based on guessing about the future. These predictions are called *ratings projections.* For an established program that has been on the air for months or years, a sales representative can create a ratings projection based on prior performance. For brand new programs with no ratings track record, this projection process is based mostly on educated guessing that takes into account, for example, previous success by the producer, director, or stars. As presented in an earlier chapter on selling audiences, guessing wrong about audience delivery can result in the network or station offering *make-good* commercials.

This looking to the future also occurs when stations purchase the broadcast rights for syndicated programming. Recall that the calculation of program revenue potential is based on anticipated ratings performance. In some cases the syndicator may offer a guarantee in which the station will pay less per episode if ratings do not achieve an agreed minimum level. Syndicated contract program renewals can also be influenced by ratings. Negotiating the value of a program for another long-term contract will inevitably include discussions about rating points and share points.

In order to better understand the exposure of commercials to audiences, advertisers and media buyers often introduce a *reach and frequency* analysis to ratings. *Reach* is defined as the number of households or people that are exposed at least once to a commercial over a specified time period. For this calculation, individual households or people are counted only once. Reach is often expressed as a percentage of the total population under study. For example, an analysis might reveal that a particular advertising campaign will reach 70 percent of the targeted population. *Frequency* is defined as the average number of times these individuals are exposed to a commercial. Returning to the prior example, we might conclude that, in addition to reaching 70 percent of our desired audience, the average number of commercial exposures will be three times; thus, the campaign generates a *frequency* of three. While the standard Nielsen ratings reports do not include reach and frequency information, specialized computer software can be purchased from Nielsen or other vendors, such as Tapscan, that calculate all kinds of reach and frequency combinations for the buyers and sellers of television audiences. Again, the evaluation of the effectiveness of an advertising campaign in terms of who was reached and how often is inexorably tied to Nielsen ratings.

An example of how audience ratings and revenue data are sometimes combined can be found in the calculation of *power ratios*. The underlying assumption is that a station's share of available advertising revenue in a market should be roughly equivalent to its share of audience. That is, a station earning a 50 percent share of audiences should also be attracting at least 50 percent of the advertising. Investors interested in purchasing radio properties often look at a station's power ratios to help estimate its market value. Additionally, station managers will look at power ratios to assess the productivity of a station's sales force. Under both circumstances, the belief is that, regardless of how big or small a station's ratings may be, it still should attract its "fair share" of advertising. Mathematically, this perfect relationship would result in a power ratio of *one*. For example, a highly successful station earning a 50 percent share of audience would be expected to draw approximately 50 percent of all television advertising (or 50 divided by 50 = 1). Similarly, a lesser station attracting only 10 percent of the available audience would be expected to earn approximately 10 percent of available advertising revenue. As a result, despite a huge difference in actual earnings, two stations could still exhibit similar power ratios, reinforcing the idea that ratings drive revenue.

The use of audience ratings is not limited to television programming and advertising professionals. Government policymakers often use audience data to justify the regulation or deregulation of certain components of the industry. For example, in the 1970s the FCC made use of ratings data to justify several rules designed to limit the influence of the Big Three networks on prime time exposure, program production, and syndication (see the Prime Time Access Rule and Financial Interest and Syndication Rules discussed in chapter 5). In recent years, ratings data have been used in policy research to analyze station ownership restrictions. In addition, ratings data concerning children's television-viewing habits have been used to substantiate the need for program content regulation. As the FCC monitors the ongoing transition from analog to digital transmission, ratings will surely play a role in assessing the distribution and popularity of HDTV and multicasting.

Now that we have a deeper understanding of how ratings are used in the industry and how important they are, we turn to some of the underlying principles of acquiring audience information from *samples*.

Sample-Based Research

In a perfect world we would conduct a *census* of every person of interest in a population, so there would be no room for statistical error in our conclusions. But in the real world, a census usually is not practical and, consequently, we opt for using representative samples. Sample-based research studies are not new and are commonly used in business and science whenever it is impractical to measure every single unit of whatever the researcher is interested in studying. For example, in order for a doctor to determine your blood type, is it necessary to drain your entire body of blood? Of course not—a simple, randomly drawn sample is sufficient. Similarly, you don't need to eat an entire pot of vegetable soup to know what kind of soup it is. A cup or even a spoonful of soup is more than adequate to represent what is in the pot, assuming beforehand that you thoroughly stir the soup to make sure the sample represents all the different ingredients. Using research terminology, the pot of soup is your statistical *population* or *universe* to be examined. The stirring process is the attempt to acquire a truly *random sample*, meaning that every item of interest within the designated population has the same chance (that is, the same mathematical probability) of being selected as every other item. In the case of audience research, a random sample means that *everybody* in a given television market has the same chance of being placed in that sample. This is not necessarily an easy promise to keep. Unlike the relative ease of acquiring a random sample of blood, or stew, imagine the challenge of drawing a random sample of a television market consisting of thousands, if not millions, of people living in a geographical area of several hundred square miles! Compounding this challenge, imagine that of the randomly selected people you approach for a study, half will refuse to participate (a problem not found among vegetables in a pot of stew). These are just some of the problems television researchers, most notably Nielsen, face in attempting to measure television audience behavior.

An important research factor often overlooked by both the general public and media professionals is that even if a researcher has the good fortune of acquiring a mathematically perfect random sample, the results are still *estimates* of what *probably* is going on in the larger population. All sample-based research should provide calculations of *sampling error* or *margins of error* and, indeed, Nielsen does caution the users of its ratings data and provides means of roughly calibrating sampling error, but the media and advertising industries seldom bother with these statistical headaches. Instead, they assume the ratings are absolute.

Another aspect of sample-based research that sometimes confuses people is that the size of the population under study has no influence on the reliability of the results of a sample taken from that population. Common sense would maintain that the bigger the sample, the more accurate the results, but people have a hard time accepting the fact that big populations do not require bigger samples than smaller populations require. From the point of view of statistics and the laws of probability, if a selected sample is truly *random*, the size of the population from which the sample is taken is not a factor in *determining the margin of error found within the results*. On the contrary, what does matter is the size of the sample itself and the degree of variability in the collected data. As perplexing as this may be for some people to grasp, this is the reason why nationwide surveys do not require huge samples. The trick is to be assured that the sample is not *biased*, meaning that indeed every member of the targeted population has an equal chance of being chosen to participate in the sample. In recent years, most criticism of Nielsen's research procedures has not been about the size of the sample but rather how representative the sample is.

Having a better appreciation of the promise and perils of sample-based research in general, let us take a closer look at how Nielsen goes about measuring television audiences.

Nielsen Media Research

In the United States, Nielsen Media Research provides television audience estimates for broadcast and cable networks, television stations, program syndicators, regional cable television systems, satellite providers, advertisers, and advertising agencies. Nielsen's corporate website provides a detailed explanation of its methodology and client offerings. For our purposes, the company's services can be divided into two groupings: national and local ratings. For both types of surveys, Nielsen recruits participants by first selecting a random sample of a designated population using updated U.S. census data and other proprietary sources that offer information on household addresses and telephone numbers. Selected households are contacted by telephone and mail. Some households are solicited for long-term meter measurement that may last several years, while others are solicited for short-term diary measurement that lasts just one week. The identities of participants are kept confidential. Of course, participating families do not have to keep it a secret, but Nielsen promises that it will not disclose the information to anyone. The following is merely a summary of available information. The Nielsen Media Research website offers more details on company history and its many products and services to clients.[3]

National Ratings

The heart of the Nielsen Media Research national ratings service in the United States is an electronic measurement system called the Nielsen *People Meter*. These meters are placed in a sample of over 5,000 households in the United States, randomly selected and recruited by Nielsen Media Research. Nielsen is gradually increasing the size of its national sample to about 15,000 homes. The People Meter is attached to each television set in the sample household. The meter measures two things— what program or channel is being tuned and who is watching. The People Meter is used to collect audience estimates for broadcast and cable networks, nationally distributed syndicated programs, and satellite distributors. Which television source is being watched in the sample homes (broadcast, cable, and so on) is continually recorded by one part of the meter, which has been calibrated to identify which station, network, or satellite is carried on each channel in the home. Channel changes are electronically monitored by the meter. Nielsen gathers information about source and time of telecast for television programs, and when this information is combined with source tuning data from their sample homes, they can "credit" audiences to specific television programs.

Exactly who is watching is measured by another component of the People Meter that uses an electronic "box" at each television set in the home and accompanying remote control units. Each family member in the sample household is assigned a personal viewing button on the People Meter. The identity, age, and sex of each person in the household are pre-set. While the television set is in use, a red light flashes periodically on the meter, reminding viewers to press their assigned buttons. Additional buttons are allocated for visitors. Information derived from these meters is accumulated daily and presented electronically to subscribing clients the next morning, hence the nickname of "overnights."

This is not a fail-safe measurement system. Sample participants can still forget or refuse to log on to the meter. Conversely, participants who leave the room might forget to log off. Because the meter doesn't know better, it will continue to record bogus "viewing" and ultimately assign rating points to the program that is on. Also, logging on does not necessarily mean that these people are attentively watching what is on the screen. In large group settings, people often become distracted and begin conversations with other people in the room. Again, the meter cannot detect this and will continue to record "viewing."

Local Ratings

For decades, electronic meters were used in only a handful of big television markets such as New York, Chicago, and Los Angeles. Gradually the top ten markets became metered, but for the rest of the country, which comprised almost two hundred individual markets, local television operators had to rely on a paper and pencil *diary system* in which participants literally wrote down their viewing habits for one week. Although this diary-based methodology is still in place, in recent years Nielsen has expanded its meters into more markets.

As of the writing of this book, fifty-six of the largest markets in the United States are now metered, although they are not using People Meters but rather a simpler device that only records set use and not viewer demographics. Consequently, only "household viewing" can be reported. Nielsen plans to upgrade these markets gradually with the more sophisticated People Meter technology, but until that time arrives, demographic information is still acquired from these markets through diaries. As with the national sample, ratings information is provided as "overnights" for these metered local markets. This information is used by local television stations, local cable systems, advertisers, and their agencies to make programming and media-buying decisions.

In each of these markets, approximately four- to five-hundred households are recruited, and electronic meters are installed on each television set in the sample home. Household tuning data from both the national and local metered samples for each day are stored in the in-home metering system until they are automatically retrieved by Nielsen computers each night. Data include when the set is turned on, which channel is tuned, when the channel is changed, when the set is off, and, for the People Meter households, who is viewing, and when that person's viewing begins and ends.

Diary measurement is used to collect viewing information from sample homes in every one of the 210 television markets in the United States in November, February, May, and July of each year. Several larger markets have two additional measurement periods, for a total of six. These four-week, diary-based measurement times are known in the industry as "the sweeps," or "sweep weeks." Remember, the majority of television markets still rely exclusively on sweeps data derived from paper diaries. Of course, most of the population of the United States is concentrated in the larger markets, so that 50 of the 210 television markets account for almost half of all U.S. households.

For meter markets not using People Meters, meaning that they cannot retrieve demographic data, diaries are used to fill this void. Standard reports statistically merge household metered data with diary-based demographic data. As a result, even though metered markets are being measured every day, the periodic "sweep weeks" are still important because of their contribution to demographic ratings.

The reliability of Nielsen's diary surveys has been questioned for decades. In addition to sampling issues discussed earlier, diary-based, or what researchers call "self-report surveys," are always vulnerable to participants' not disclosing the truth, either deliberately or by accident.

For example, although Nielsen instructs participants to fill out their diaries every day, research has found that most people wait until the last day and then attempt to recall all their viewing episodes for the entire week. Needless to say, even with the best of intentions, people can make mistakes when asked to have perfect recall. Another problem is that people lie. They either fail to mention a particular program because they are embarrassed, or, conversely, they mention a favorite program that in reality they were unavailable to watch that specific week. Regardless, they enter into their diaries a phony viewing episode. Most media researchers are convinced that meters are more trustworthy than diaries.

Another nagging problem that has only become worse in recent years has been the poor cooperation rates among people who are initially approached by Nielsen to become diary participants. This problem is sometimes referred to as *nonresponse error.* Today, fewer than 50 percent of the people asked actually agree to participate. As a result, Nielsen must "over-sample" a market in order to obtain a large-enough sample to be reasonably reliable. *Buffer samples* are lists of additional households that have been randomly generated and held in reserve in case the original sampling recruitment fails to reach expectations. Certain age, sex, and ethnic groups are particularly troublesome. For instance, in some markets young Hispanic males are difficult to persuade. Because nonresponse error has the potential to bias the ratings, this is a serious threat to the accuracy of these reports. Cash incentives are used to encourage cooperation, but these inducements still are not sufficient to offset the demographic voids in some market samples. A solution has been *statistical weighting* (sometimes called *sample balancing*), a mathematical procedure applied to the data after it has been collected, intended to give more ratings "weight" to demographic groups that are not properly represented. Statistical weighting is common among many types of marketing and political research studies. A simple example would be a sample that requires 50 percent men and 50 percent women to match the known proportions of the specific population under study. A researcher attempts to obtain a random sample but discovers that for some reason he or she has a working sample of 40 percent men and 60 percent women. One solution to this quandary would be to go back in the field and recruit more men, but a more common solution is to mathematically adjust or weight the responses of these people to create the proper balance. In other words, in this particular sample the response of men would be counted more than once. Each male response would be multiplied by a factor of 10 percent to make up for the difference between the 40 percent recruited and the 50 percent desired. Although Nielsen insists that these manipulated samples still accurately represent the larger population under study, critics worry that people who refuse to participate may have different television viewing habits than people who willingly volunteer. They maintain that over-sampling and statistical weighting do not solve this problem. For television markets that have considerable Hispanic populations, such as Miami, Los Angeles, and San Antonio, this sampling issue has generated heated debates between Nielsen and station operators.

As a means of testing the accuracy of its standard meter and diary research formats, Nielsen regularly conducts *telephone coincidentals*. In these tests, they call thousands of randomly selected telephone numbers and ask people what program they are watching right at that moment. This research provides a completely independent check on the amount of television use and viewing choices, and when they have found some differences, it has helped them to zero in on ways to improve measurement techniques. Nielsen uses multiple methods—meters, diaries, and telephone coincidentals—to continually cross-check the reliability of its surveys. Although each method has its advantages and disadvantages for measuring audience *exposure*, none can confirm that a participant is truly *paying attention* to a program or commercial.

Time-shifted programs (namely, digital video recordings, or DVRs) are now included in Nielsen's metered surveys. The company is experimenting with reporting protocols that would reflect (a) live viewing, (b) recorded and viewed same-day, and (c) recorded and viewed within one week. This type of viewing breakout is of particular interest to advertisers attempting to sell time-sensitive products and services, such as special promotions or sales. Television sales executives are less enthusiastic, fearing that media buyers will ask for commercial rate reductions or *make-goods* after the fact during *post-analysis* (see chapter 3 on selling audiences). Imagine in the near future a commercial agreement with an advertiser that guarantees not just bulk ratings but a specified number of same-day viewing ratings!

Identifying Television Programs and Commercials

Nielsen's primary source of information about which programs are airing for each station or cable channel comes from a very special, coded ID number that is part of almost every television picture—a series of lines and dots at the top edge of the picture that labels the program and episode. These patented systems, called AMOL, or Automated Measurement of Line-ups, consist of sites located across the country, where television stations are monitored and the program ID codes are analyzed. Each night, these monitoring sites connect up to a central computer and download the information. Nielsen compiles the electronic program information and compares it to other sources of information they have already received. If they detect discrepancies, they call television stations and cable operators to verify what actually was aired.

In addition to identifying television programs, Nielsen also keeps track of thousands of commercials. National advertisers in particular are interested in this service as a way of making sure that their commercials were aired properly in dozens, if not hundreds, of markets. Using special passive television signal identification technology, commercials on television stations are continuously monitored and converted into a digital "fingerprint." These fingerprints are then compared to a computer file of fingerprints from thousands of different commercials and automatically identified. This information is used to produce reports detailing when and where television commercials actually aired. Similar to its business model for audience ratings, Nielsen charges clients a subscriber fee for access to this program and commercial information.

The Future of Audience Measurement

New technology breakthroughs have enabled research companies to introduce more exotic ways to record audience behavior. For its home-based meters, Nielsen's research and development engineers have been experimenting with scanning devices that can recognize faces and conduct simple oral "conversations" with participants, such as confirming their names and asking what program they are watching. The company is also looking at the prospect of utilizing inexpensive "mailable meters" that can be distributed and returned through the mail and then reused for another survey.

One of the more promising instruments is being tested by a strategic partnership between former rivals Nielsen Media Research and the Arbitron Company. The product is called the Portable People Meter, or PPM. Since 1992, the patented audio encoding system has been continuously improved, tested, and refined and is now ready for deployment in ongoing audience measurement research. It provides an extremely reliable means of identifying signal source and works equally well with all existing electronic media delivery systems: analog, digital, live, and recorded broadcasts. The embedded codes can even be picked up in transmissions delivered through the Internet.

The Portable People Meter is a unique audience measurement system that tracks what consumers listen to on the radio and what consumers watch on broadcast television, cable, and satellite television. The PPM is a mobile-phone-sized device that consumers wear throughout the day. It works by detecting identification codes that can be embedded in the audio portion of any transmission. Nielsen's current fixed metering system does not include out-of-home viewing locations, such as dormitories, barracks, hospitals, and taverns. This portable system for broadcasting can record activity almost anywhere. The PPM consists of several components:

- An *encoder* installed at the radio or television station that inserts an inaudible identification code into the audio portion of the program content.
- Individual *Portable People Meters* worn by sample participants to detect and record the inaudible codes in the programming.
- A *base station* where each survey participant places the meter at

the end of the day to recharge the battery and send collected codes to a household data collection device known as a "hub."

According to Arbitron, which actually invented the device, the PPM is designed to meet the challenges of digital and satellite broadcasting as well as the convergence of media and the Internet. No matter where the survey participant listens to the radio or watches television, the meter can capture and report the media exposure. Because an inaudible program code stays embedded in the audio even after a program is recorded on a VCR or digital recorder such as TiVo or Replay, the PPM can capture and identify station exposure no matter what methods of recording and play-back are used. Instead of today's mix of immobile electronic meters attached to home sets and cumbersome personal diaries, the PPM can be the common audience measurement tool for all the local electronic media.[4]

The PPM is not a perfect device for recoding audience behavior. Researchers have found problems with overlapping signals, where the meter cannot pick up precisely several stations operating simultaneously within the reception radius of the meter. Also, if a person is wearing a headset or ear buds, the PMM will probably not detect the listening episode. Finally, early tests have found disappointing cooperation rates. Apparently many people, especially women, do not like to wear such a conspicuous device. Because the above-mentioned methodological problems and other business considerations, in 2006 Nielsen ended its PPM partnership with Arbitron. However, as of the writing of this text, Arbitron promises to continue work on its device for radio and insinuates that it still might go after television and cable measurement business as a rival for Nielsen.

Most media researchers would agree that the more "passive" the measuring device, the more accurate the results. That is, the more that volunteers have to actively chronicle their program choices, like pushing a button or writing something down, the less exact the information about audience behavior will be. Of course, accuracy is also a function of reliable sampling techniques, on which the PPM technology has no influence.

Although Nielsen is the dominant provider of television audience information, we would be wrong to presume that it is the only provider. Today several other well-respected companies offer valuable information about audience behavior and attitudes. Most are marketing firms that study consumer demographics, lifestyles, and buying habits, and merge this information with "media usage" data. Some of the more prominent firms are the Claritas Company, Mediamark Research, Scarborough Research, and Simmons Market Research. These companies all have websites offering detailed information on their specific services.

Perhaps the most provocative source of future competition for Nielsen is the ability of the cable industry to acquire a true *census* of viewing behavior with no need to wrestle with the inherent problems of sampling error and response error. Several large cable companies, together with some research entrepreneurs, are looking seriously at the ability of interactive digital cable to monitor the viewing of all subscribers. Right now, digital cable is still expanding and therefore cannot reflect the habits of all viewers, but at the very least media executives could get an accurate reading on all digital subscribers, which is substantial and growing. From a business perspective, this "wired" approach could bypass Nielsen altogether or, more likely, encourage Nielsen to become an active partner in the venture. Lurking nearby are critics who do not like the circumstances of a kind of "Big Brother" electronically eavesdropping on peoples' private media habits. They argue that, unlike this proposed cable method, Nielsen's metered and diary-based surveys still require the *informed consent* of sample participants. So, while the technology of acquiring close to a true census is not that far away, the regulatory implications concerning invasion of privacy may blossom into a major debate. The cable industry maintains fervently that during data processing the information would be "scrambled," so that viewing could not be traced back to individuals or households. Of course, this is a matter of ethics and people doing the right thing. An unscrupulous company might "forget" to scramble the personal data, and the subscribers would never know the difference.

On a typical weeknight, over 100 million Americans watch prime time programming. The average household, now with access to more than one hundred channels, sees slightly more than eight hours of television every day on several different sets often tuned to different program sources. Additionally, many programs are not viewed when scheduled but recorded and time-shifted for hours or days. Furthermore, television programming can now be downloaded to home computer screens, portable iPods, and cell phones. In coming years, keeping track of who is watching what at what time and on what type of device will be a daunting challenge for the television industry.

For readers desiring a deeper understanding of this industry topic, the definitive book on ratings research is *Ratings Analysis; The Theory and Practice of Audience Research.*[5]

 ## Questions for Further Thought

1   In your opinion, how would *competition* in the television ratings business affect the system of the television industry?

2   Provide examples of sample-based research used by other types of businesses and government agencies.

3   Would you be willing to wear a Portable People Meter (PPM) every day for a week? Explain your answer in some detail.

4   Can you think of an audience-measuring device that would be superior to the PPM?

5   Do you believe that the newly proposed digital cable monitoring device that could measure the viewing behavior of all subscribers is an invasion of privacy? Explain your answer in some detail.

The Lessons of History

DuMont, Fox and the Quest for a Fourth Network

The introduction of this book proposed a systems approach to better understand the inner workings of the television industry, acknowledging that the essential business of television involves an intermingling of technology, regulation, and economics. In addition, this intermingling has a history, wherein the past has set the stage for the future. A case study that exemplifies these factors is a brief retelling of the industry's attempts to create and sustain a fourth network. The story has two main characters, the DuMont network and the Fox network. Each, in its own era, attempted to break the dominance of the entrenched Big Three networks of ABC, CBS, and NBC. The first attempt, launched in 1948, failed miserably, while the second, launched in 1986, succeeded superbly. No single positive or negative factor determined the demise of one or the rise of the other. Instead, a combination of factors brought about these final outcomes.

In 1955, Alan B. DuMont was caught in the crosshairs of history, where the juxtaposition of unproven technology, frustrating government regulation, and a ruthless economic environment created a recipe for disaster not only for his namesake network but also for the development of UHF television for the next thirty years. Conversely, in 1987, Rupert Murdoch found that the same intertwined factors had evolved into far-less-threatening circumstances for a network challenger. In other words, the *system* had changed. The goal of this chapter is not only to present the facts of what happened but also to foster a better understanding of the complexity of the media industry and how the system changes over time. Having read the earlier chapters of this book, the reader will have a better appreciation of some of the components of this story.

In the Beginning

As early as 1931, Alan B. DuMont, Ph.D., saw the promise of television when he resigned from the De Forest Radio Company and opened his own experimental laboratory in a basement garage in Upper Montclair, New Jersey. With $1,000 in capital and three assistants, he developed the first commercially practical cathode ray tube. The subsequent DuMont Laboratories and its subsidiaries became principal manufacturers of vacuum tubes, studio cameras, television sets, transmitters, and other related electronic gear. Profits from these manufacturing endeavors were diverted toward the acquisition and operation of television stations.

In 1938, seeking funding beyond his own company, DuMont struck a fateful deal with Paramount Pictures, whereby in exchange for considerable cash, the movie studio was essentially given half ownership of the company through the purchase of common stock. This partnership in a burgeoning business would prove to be a very one-sided financial relationship, in which for years Paramount would exploit DuMont for impressive profits, while refusing to invest an additional dime beyond its initial 1938 stock purchase. Like many of today's "strategic alliances," the partners became embroiled in boardroom power struggles.

In 1939, DuMont's first experimental television station (W2XWV) went on the air in Passaic, New Jersey. That same year, at the New York World's Fair, DuMont demonstrated the first television sets for sale to the general public. By 1941, NBC, CBS, and DuMont were all operating experimental VHF stations in the New York City area.

The momentum was weakened by World War II (1941–45). At the end of the war, there were only six surviving experimental television outlets in the entire country, but the stature of television would soon change dramatically. With the war restriction lifted, commercial license applications to the Federal Communications Commission soared. In 1945, the FCC established a table of television channel assignments for the country, but the demand for access to the VHF spectrum far exceeded the government's expectations. During this time, the commission gave DuMont's experimental station in New York a commercial license and a new set of call letters, WABD. In April 1946, DuMont acquired his second VHF station in Washington, DC, with the call letters WTTG. A year later, in 1947, the FCC granted an application for a third DuMont VHF station in Pittsburgh with the call letters WDTV.

By 1947, with three stations and an AT&T coaxial cable interconnection in place, Dr. DuMont announced at the company's annual stockholders' meeting his intention to form a full-fledged television network consisting of stations owned by DuMont, plus several station affiliates located in major cities.

During this time, the demand for station licenses was overwhelming. In order to study the problem properly, the FCC in 1948 instituted a temporary "freeze" on all station applications. What was intended to take only a few months actually took almost four years. During this time, all four networks posted losses, but 1950 was the last year that DuMont remained on a financial par with its competitors. Beginning in 1951, the network would register ever-increasing losses, while NBC, CBS, and ABC would show revenue gains each year despite the freeze.

By dawdling for years on this issue, the FCC accelerated the fall of DuMont. Not only did NBC and CBS control far more stations during these years, but they also had the added advantage of brand recognition. From decades of exposure on the radio, audiences and advertisers trusted these familiar media brands, which led to enhanced ratings and revenue. Most early VHF television affiliations were with established radio-station operators with the same network affiliation. Often, the same station management and sales staff worked for both radio and television. Alan DuMont, on the other hand, was essentially an unknown and, therefore, had to work that much harder to legitimize his network with audiences and advertisers.

During the 1948–1952 freeze, DuMont took an active role in offering proposals for the commission's master allocation plan. Believing that UHF stations would have a distinct signal disadvantage compared to VHF, he proposed that all channels be UHF, relinquishing the VHF spectrum to other communications. This is similar to the current digital conversion plan whereby stations are eventually supposed to relinquish their analog channels back to the FCC for other uses, most notably wireless communication.

Another alternative proposal made by DuMont recommended that individual markets be either all UHF or all VHF, thus leveling the playing field on a market-by-market basis. Later, he proposed a third option in which the nation's fifty biggest markets would be assigned a minimum of five VHF channels, with smaller markets receiving only UHF allocations. From a revenue standpoint, it was essential that DuMont be in the biggest markets with a competitive signal. He claimed that the worst scenario would be to have "intermixed" VHF and UHF markets where UHF stations could not compete effectively. In April 1952, DuMont's worst fears came true. The FCC Sixth Report and Order endorsed the notion of intermixing UHF with VHF. The problem was that CBS and NBC had already established VHF affiliations prior to the freeze, essentially forcing DuMont to struggle with mostly UHF stations.

Coping with Unproven Technologies

Given the receiving equipment at the time, watching UHF television in the 1950s was an ordeal even under the best of circumstances. When the 1952 Sixth Report and Order was made law, there was not a single UHF transmitter or UHF home receiver in the country. UHF was an unproven technology intended to resolve the ever-growing demand for television station licenses. Although DuMont conducted a few experiments with UHF reception with disturbing results, there is no record that the government conducted any type of comprehensive studies with this new technology. The FCC's optimistic belief in the technical viability of UHF television was based more on wishful thinking than on clinical trails.

DuMont Perseveres

In the early 1950s, the demand among entrepreneurs for UHF channel licenses was huge, and DuMont remained financially solvent by selling UHF transmitters to station operators and home receivers to the general public. But while the number of new sign-on stations was high, the rate of attrition was even higher. For example, in 1954, twenty-five new UHF stations went on the air, but in that same year, twenty-nine other UHF stations ceased operations. This trend of more stations stopping rather than starting operations each year buttressed DuMont's dire predictions that UHF simply could not compete.

Television Audiences Become Selective

The introduction of television was enormously popular from the very beginning. During the early 1950s, television set manufacturers could barely keep up with consumer demand. However, the novelty of television gave way quickly to audience preference for specific programs.

While DuMont had some modest program successes, such as *Captain Video*, *The Original Amateur Hour*, and *Cavalcade of Stars* starring Jackie Gleason, it could not compete head-to-head with the programming blockbusters on competing networks, such as the *Texaco Star Theater* with Milton Berle and the legendary *I Love Lucy*. Furthermore, many rising DuMont stars, such as Gleason, abruptly changed networks when NBC or CBS offered more money. Television production was expensive, and DuMont stations were hemorrhaging red ink. Cost cutting led to lackluster program content, which translated into equally lackluster ratings. Of course, expensive productions do not guarantee ratings success, but DuMont was punished economically by having successful program producers and talent defect to competing networks. After 1950, the network never had a prime-time program ranked among the top twenty-five. The cost of doing business has always been a major concern for television networks. Today, in order to retain a long-running hit program, the networks often are coerced by producers and production studios to pay exorbitant licensing fees representing millions of dollars per episode.

The Dike Breaks

By 1953 the DuMont network was in serious financial trouble. As one DuMont executive put it, "The dike was crumbling and we didn't have enough thumbs. . . ."[1] Although in the beginning all four networks endured heavy loses, by the early 1950s both CBS and NBC were registering respectable profits. DuMont, however, continued down the slippery slope of financial ruin. Alan DuMont's management strategies shifted from a *proactive* posture, where he was hoping to capture a place at the table with the Big Three networks, to a *reactive* posture, where he was working desperately to keep "thumbs in the dike" of a crumbling UHF network. Cost cutting to the bone may have hurt the network even more in that production values were often sacrificed at the expense of compelling program content. In 1954, DuMont entered into a contract with Westinghouse Broadcasting to sell WDTV Pittsburgh for $9,750,000. Although the sale generated needed cash, the loss of one of the DuMont flagship stations sent a message to the broadcasting and advertising industries that the condition of the DuMont network was terminal. On 10 October 1955, the DuMont television network signed off the air for the last time. Alan B. DuMont died in 1965. A decade later, television set manufacturers finally were mandated by the FCC to produce VHF-UHF compatible units.

Multiple decisions contained within the FCC's 1952 Sixth Report and Order had dire consequences on the network's ability to compete effectively against CBS and NBC. As discussed in prior sections, the geographical intermixture of VHF and UHF channel allocations resulted in CBS and NBC having a huge advantage in signal transmission and reception. The inability of DuMont to achieve a strong UHF presence in major markets caused the network to be less attractive to advertisers, which resulted in the predictable symptoms of disappointing commercial rates and unrealized sales budgets. Decades later, in 1982, the FCC belatedly confessed that UHF television was a technological nightmare.

> The growth of the UHF service has been tumultuous to say the least . . . stations must broadcast at higher and more costly power levels to achieve coverage similar to VHF stations; and UHF frequencies are more attenuated by natural obstacles such as terrain and foliage. In addition, television receivers have not always provided equivalent tuning and reception of UHF and VHF stations.[2]

Fox Prevails

In December 1955, the DuMont-owned stations were severed from the parent DuMont Laboratories and given a new name, Metropolitan Broadcasting. In 1959 the stations were sold outright to a company that would eventually become Metromedia.

From the demise of the DuMont television network in 1955 though the early 1980s, there were a few meager attempts to establish a fourth network, but none succeeded. In 1986, Rupert Murdoch decided that the time was ripe for another assault on the Big Three. With viewer ratings slipping away to cable, the management of the three established networks appeared to be in disarray and, therefore, vulnerable to attack. Murdoch recognized the risks but was willing to accept huge financial losses over the short term in order to create a new network.

The groundwork for the launch of the Fox network began with Murdoch's News Corporation's purchase of the 20th Century Fox movie studio. Unlike DuMont's toxic relationship with Paramount Pictures, the Fox acquisition brought needed cash and, most important, a recognizable brand name to the new network. That same year, in an ironic twist of broadcasting history, Murdoch purchased six of the former DuMont-owned stations to form the backbone of the second coming of a fourth network. Hitting the air in the fall of 1987, the Fox network included 108 affiliates, composed mostly of UHF stations.

From the beginning, Fox established itself as a somewhat edgy, irreverent, youth-oriented network compared to its rivals. Fox also took advantage of its namesake Hollywood production studio 20th Century Fox (later shortened to 20th Century). DuMont should have capitalized on its partnership with Paramount Pictures, but the partnership was in name only. Although the network created several prime-time successes, including *Married with Children, The Simpsons, Beverly Hills 90210, America's Most Wanted,* and *The X-Files,* it still languished in fourth place. Furthermore, unlike DuMont, the Fox network did not overextend itself with too many programs. Daytime hours and weekends were ignored completely so that the network could focus on establishing a beachhead in prime time.

Part of Murdock's master plan for upgrading the Fox network was not only to develop unique programming but also to acquire more major-market VHF station affiliates. Of course, this meant that he was willing to abandon any current UHF Fox affiliates that got in the way. Murdoch's first assault occurred in 1993 when he purchased twelve successful VHF stations from New World Communications with the understanding that all stations would forsake their current network affiliations to ABC, CBS, and NBC and join the Fox network family of stations as soon as legally possible. In coming years, Murdoch purchased additional major-market stations and also persuaded dozens of other stations to switch affiliations. In 1994, Fox enhanced its reputation dramatically by outbidding CBS for NFL football rights. Over the next decade, the decades-old industry jargon of "The Big Three" networks gave way to "The Big Four" networks. With the 2004–5 season, Fox was beating all three of its rivals in audience delivery of the highly coveted 18–49 age group.

So why did Fox prevail as America's fourth network when DuMont thirty years earlier had failed so miserably?

First, by the mid 1980s, independent UHF television had grown into a mature business, surviving on proven counter-programming strategies that emphasized children's programming, movies, and sports. Many stations had been on the air for over twenty years, and the industry had groomed a generation of experienced managers. Second, UHF technology had come a long way since the 1950s. Station transmitters were more powerful and, more important, all home television sets could now receive UHF channels. Had the physics of over-the-air television not been so troublesome, the DuMont saga might have had a happier ending.

As shown earlier in this book, cable television was more of a benefactor than a competitor for most UHF stations during the 1980s. The FCC "Must Carry" rules mandated that cable systems must carry all local stations operating in the cable franchise area. This lessened greatly the chronic over-the-air reception problems, particularly for distant communities that could only receive VHF signals clearly.

During this same era, the FCC granted several important business concessions to UHF stations, including exclusion from the Prime Time Access Rules (PTAR), which forbade stations in the top fifty markets from airing off-network syndicated programs between 7:00 and 8:00 PM. Also, ownership limits for UHF stations were modified so that a group could legally hold twice as many UHF stations as VHF stations. This supposed strength-in-numbers philosophy would help sustain struggling stations and stimulate investment.

Murdoch was also shrewd enough to realize that a new network would need to offer truly unique program content. Many industry observers credit Fox for being the first network to develop a distinctive brand image. Its irreverent, youth-oriented programs, such *as Married with Children*, would reaffirm the network's intention of becoming an obvious programming alternative for audiences and advertisers. Capitalizing on the highly recognizable Fox brand name was also no accident. DuMont never had an overarching programming strategy that would position his network as truly different compared to his three competitors. Also, the DuMont name meant little or nothing to the general public.

The Fox network also had the financial advantage of an owner with deep pockets. In addition to providing much-needed capital for internal network operation, Murdoch also tempted stations to switch affiliations by offering substantially higher network compensation fees than what the Big Three were offering affiliates. Murdoch's numerous holdings in the print media and movie studios enabled him to absorb network losses that for many years totaled in the hundreds of millions of dollars. Unlike DuMont, who relinquished much managerial control to Paramount Pictures in exchange for needed cash, Murdoch kept all transactions under his decision-making authority. He continued to be the primary decision maker as the network grew and prospered. In summary, the interaction of managerial experience, friendlier technology, cable retransmission, strategic programming, and a willingness to invest for the long term enabled Fox to establish itself as a competitive fourth network. However, the stigma of UHF would remain.

Fast Forward to the Twenty-First Century

As with the introduction of UHF in the 1950s, the FCC has great expectations for the development of digital television in the new millennium. In addition to wide-screen HDTV, broadcasters will have the option of multicasting several conventional channels, which, in turn, can be organized into new networks. Mirroring the situation of DuMont and the introduction of UHF many years ago, the distant horizon looks promising, but the more immediate practical concerns appear mired in consumer confusion and business indifference. The exact deadline for starting full digital transmissions (while shutting down all analog broadcasting) has been debated and delayed several times. Truly pessimistic industry observers compare the digital changeover to the adoption of color television, which took twenty years to reach a national household penetration of only 50 percent. Other experts are more optimistic, expecting a sudden surge in interest within the next couple of years.

While everybody agrees that the enhanced picture quality offered by HDTV is wonderful, no one has found a persuasive business model that enables broadcasters to *make money* from this new technology. Compounding the problem is that cable operators are in no hurry to add bandwidth-guzzling HDTV signals. Broadcasters see more business potential with standard television multi-casting options, but with over 85 percent of the nation subscribing to cable and satellite, multicasting must be embraced by these non-broadcast technologies. Meanwhile, amid this industry turmoil, most of the general public hasn't a clue as to what digital television really is. Retailers have yet to experience hordes of eager customers wishing to spend thousands of dollars on new digital receivers.

Learning from History

As a business case study, DuMont's struggle with UHF seemed for many years to be a story relegated to the dusty shelves of ancient history, but with the mandated introduction of digital television, the network's ordeal with "new technology" offers some contemporary insights.

First, unproven technologies often require a period of trial and error. As exemplified by DuMont's struggle with UHF, the current digital transition will probably take much longer than anticipated and will encounter complex reception hurdles along the way. This does not imply that DTV is a bad idea. On the contrary, the conversion is necessary and inevitable, but the implementation will require patience and fortitude.

Second, the speed of this digital conversion will depend in large part on reconciling the role of government policy in influencing the private sector. Over the years, the philosophical pendulum has swung back and forth several times, all in the name of the public interest. For DuMont, the agonizingly slow development of UHF can be attributed to frustrating government policy that, after creating a debilitating VHF-UHF intermixed channel allocation system, was unwilling to rectify the problem in a decisive and timely manner. Today, despite an open-market deregulatory posture on the part of the current White House and the FCC, the digital conversion appears to need continued government prodding to get broadcasters and set manufacturers to invest in this new technology.

Third, broadcast digital television will never succeed without the endorsement of the cable and satellite services. They must agree to provide the needed bandwidth to accommodate wide-screen HDTV plus an array of standard television multi-cast niche channels. In the past, cable has been both friend and foe to the television broadcaster, and the future looks equally ambiguous.

Finally, the core reason for the obvious lack of enthusiasm for the digital conversion is more economic than technological. To date, nobody has put forth a business model that projects a substantial profit to be made from going digital. For decades, DuMont in particular and UHF television in general were shunned by investors and advertisers because they did not make good business sense. Similarly, the purported wonders of digital television must be witnessed not only on the television screen but also on the bottom line. Furthermore, digital entrepreneurs must remember that people watch programs, not technology. DuMont realized quickly that the novelty of new technology soon gives way to audience demand for specific content. Aside from affluent early-adopters, who buy new technology merely for the sake of technology itself, the only way the larger American public will become enthusiastic about digital television is through compelling program content. Just as ordinary Americans in the 1950s were reluctant to discard their VHF-only televisions in favor of more expensive all-channel receivers, Americans today must be persuaded that digital television is worth their investment.

The demise of DuMont and the rise of Fox are more than obscure topics for television history buffs. The quest for a fourth network is also a worthwhile case study for pondering our digital future. Given the benefit of hindsight, we can see "obvious" problems lurking around the introduction of UHF in the 1950s, but at the time the facts were not at all clear. Similarly, people may look back at our current era and marvel at how ill-prepared we were for the transition to digital. Only time will tell. We can, however, use history to illuminate how, over the long run, the television industry functions, fails, adapts, and evolves. In addition, we can see the intermingling of technology, regulation, and economics. For example, in the beginning, the *economic* demand for more station licenses, coupled with the *technological* constraints of a limited spectrum, led to a *regulatory* response from the FCC in introducing the untried technology of UHF, which in turn had an awful impact on the *economics* of UHF station operators and the DuMont network. Eventually, the regulators recognized the full extent of the technological shortcomings of UHF and mandated *economic* reforms for television set manufacturers to produce VHF-UHF-compatible units. Unfortunately, by this time DuMont was long gone. Although most historians believe the commission was simply overly optimistic and naïve about the prospects of UHF, others take a more suspicious view, insinuating that CBS and NBC sabotaged DuMont's pleas for regulatory help with backdoor payoffs and perks for key commissioners. We will never know for sure.[3] In a kind of "natural selection" predicament, DuMont could not adapt to its harsh surroundings. Too little, too late, equals system failure.

Thirty years later, Fox comes on the scene when the technological, economic, and regulatory environment of the industry is far more conducive to sustaining new life forms. Fox took advantage of a more mature industry that had overcome much of the reception handicaps of UHF reception. Add some sympathetic FCC regulations giving UHF stations some economic boost, and a new, fourth network emerges from the cold ashes of the Dumont fiasco. Harmonious conditions equal system success.

In both of these cases it is difficult to isolate factors without acknowledging the context or system in which the factor must operate. In many instances we are dealing not with direct effects but *reciprocal effects* in which one factor is reacting to the actions of another factor. For example, the FCC doesn't function in a vacuum. Instead, it attempts to respond to the needs of the industry and the public. Similarly, we can argue that new technologies are seldom developed without a corresponding economic motive. From laptop computers and cell phones to iPods and HDTV, somebody is trying to make a buck. When the marketplace can't resolve an obvious foul, government often steps in to enforce fair play. For DuMont, the government waited too long. For Fox, the government was there all the way.

 Questions and Exercises

1   Pretend you could go back in time and change history. What *one factor* in the DuMont story would you alter that might have saved the struggling network?

2   Suppose you had the opportunity to invest in a new *multicast network* that would depend on persuading one station in each television market in the country to contribute a digital sub-channel to the project. Looking back at the histories of the DuMont and Fox networks and looking forward to the growth of digital television (DTV), what technological, economic, and regulatory challenges need to be addressed for the network to become a reality?

A Troubled Relationship

Stations and Networks
Try to Work Together

While the DuMont versus Fox case study showed how the broadcasting system changes over time, this chapter takes a closer look at the sometimes-rocky relationship between television stations and their networks. Where the DuMont and Fox networks and their affiliated stations essentially pulled together to sustain a new, struggling enterprise, today's station-network relationship is under increasing stress.

This discussion was not included as part of an earlier chapter because the topic lends itself to a separate treatment in that it serves as a bellwether for the future. Just as the ripples from a pebble dropped into a pond radiate in ever-widening circles, so the issues surrounding the station-network relationship resonate with so many important challenges facing the television industry both today and in the future. The recent creation of the CW network as a replacement for the UPN and WB networks is a perfect example of the volatility of the television industry. With little prior notice, many station affiliates have been forced to become independents in the wake of the consolidated CW enterprise.

For decades, the synergistic relationship between the television networks and their affiliated stations was a marriage made in heaven, but by the 1990s the partnership was filled with dissention. Neither side was prepared to dismantle the union completely, but as one industry reporter observed, the participants looked like "two people in a donkey costume . . . not always going in the same direction, but both trying to get to the same place."[1] The fundamental problem was that while the stations were getting rich, the networks were somehow losing money. After more than a half century of success, how did the concept of network broadcasting suddenly seem like a bad idea? The origins of the answer can be found in the manner in which the affiliate relationship was first conceived. Therefore, we will begin this chapter by looking back briefly at the factors that served as catalysts for developing this relationship. We will then chronicle how this once-cozy relationship began to unravel in the 1990s as the networks' costs soared and ratings dived. Finally, we will examine emerging network program distribution ideas that over time may place the station-network partnership in more jeopardy.

Looking Back

As discussed in earlier chapters, the concept of networking made sense in the early development of radio and television. National advertisers were eager to reach huge national audiences, and local stations appreciated the quality programming and the opportunity to insert local commercials, called adjacencies, inside network programs. From a technological perspective, the only means of achieving this national exposure was to create partnerships with hundreds of stations, each broadcasting over the air to a designated geographical market. In order for affiliates to receive programming, stations were linked by wire to their parent networks. Recognizing the social and political power of network programming, the FCC from the beginning has been reluctant to have too many of these connected stations owned by the networks themselves. Instead, the commission wanted these stations to be somewhat autonomous. This technological and economic interdependency lasted for several decades, but, as we will see later on, new technologies, particularly cable and satellite delivery, and new economic realities have caused the networks to be less obligated to their partnered stations.

In an effort to encourage diversity in media ownership, the FCC in the 1940s initiated a station ownership limit of no more than five stations. With such a rule in place, the route to economic power in the television industry shifted from station ownership to station *affiliation*. Ownership restrictions have been altered several times over the decades, but the underlying legal and philosophical rationales have not changed a great deal. As elaborated in our earlier chapter on regulation, the basic rationale for such limitations is that concentration of media ownership among a few individuals or a few companies is not in the public interest.

The majority of television stations in the United States are group-owned, meaning that they are owned by a company that operates several stations. A more detailed discussion of ownership limitations was presented in the chapter addressing regulation, but for this discussion of the station-network relationship, the reader should be aware that today many important station management decisions are made on a group or corporate level. These include group purchases of syndicated programs and group affiliation renewals with the networks. Obviously, this process is much more efficient when the group owns stations affiliated with the same network, but this is not always the case. Some group owners operate stations affiliated with a variety of networks.[2] The most powerful group owners are the networks with stations licensed to the country's biggest television markets. In recent years, the networks have asked to increase the number of their owned-and-operated (O&O) stations in order to cover a greater percentage of U.S. households.

In addition to ownership issues, the FCC over the years has always been on the lookout for situations where the networks might exert too much power over their affiliated stations. As early as 1941, with what the commission called its Chain Broadcasting Rules, the FCC forbade affiliation contracts from forcing stations to carry any particular program. Ultimately, the station is responsible for the content it disseminates. For example, recent actions involving indecency on network programs have resulted in suits being filed against individual stations, not the networks per se. Of course, the networks also own many stations, and therefore legal issues involving network program content inevitably include the network's O&O stations as well.

Although the vast majority of network programs are cleared by affiliates, there are situations in which stations refuse or preempt a certain program or movie. In recent years, the reasons for this have typically been excessive sexual content, offensive racial depictions, or disrespect to religious characters. Of course, stations also have a history of preempting network programming not because of serious moral issues, but merely because the program was not popular. Chapter 3 briefly touched on this and the fallout that can occur among network advertisers. This type of preemption was far more common in the 1970s and '80s, but as renewal contracts were renegotiated in the 1990s, the networks began to play hardball with their affiliates, threatening cutbacks in compensation and other economic punishments for excessive preemptions.

In the 1960s and '70s, the FCC became concerned about the power of the networks over programming and consequently enacted both the

Prime Time Access Rule (PTAR) and the Network Financial and Syndication Rules (Fin-Syn). PTAR limited the amount of network programming and off-network syndicated programming per night to three hours in the top fifty television markets, allowing stations to schedule local or syndicated programs in the early evening hours (usually 7:00–8:00 PM). This rule was intended to stimulate alternative programming and, surprisingly, the networks relinquished this air time without much of a fight. Network executives saw the cutback in time as an opportunity to rein in ever-rising prime time production expenses. At the same time, local stations welcomed the chance to insert more commercial avails in prime time, even if now they had to pay for the programming. Today the 7:00–8:00 PM *prime access* time period for most stations is a valuable profit center. In 1995, after the old three-network oligopoly had become only a memory because of the dramatic increase in program competition, especially by the cable industry, PTAR was eliminated. Although this prime hour is no longer the exclusive domain of local stations and technically "up for grabs," the networks have made no serious attempts at recapturing the time from their affiliates.

The Fin-Syn rules addressed limiting network ownership of its own programming and forbade networks from program syndication in the United States. Again, the intent was to stimulate independent program production. Furthermore, local stations would not be pressured to buy syndicated programs from their parent network. As with PTAR, these rules were eventually phased out in the mid 1990s because of increased market competition. Ownership restrictions, Chain Broadcasting Rules, PTAR, and the Fin-Syn rules were all examples of the FCC's attempt to encourage localism, diversity, and competition within the free market.[3] In particular, these rules tried to create some kind of economic balance between the interests of stations and the interests of networks.

The Partnership

Under the conventional affiliation agreement, the affiliated stations received free programming in exchange for providing national distribution for network commercials. To sweeten the deal, the affiliated stations were given (a) cash compensation and (b) opportunities to insert local commercials (adjacencies). As a result, stations rarely changed affiliations, and when changes did occur, they were usually prompted by a network seeking a more powerful station. As might be expected, UHF stations were the most vulnerable because of their inherently poor signal reception. During the late 1970s, when ABC finally reached prime time ratings parity with CBS and NBC, there was a flurry of affiliation changes in which many VHF stations jumped ship after ABC tempted them with huge cash compensation deals.[4] Again, in the early 1990s, station affiliation changes went into a temporary frenzy as the burgeoning Fox network went trolling for VHF stations to bolster its station line-up.[5] Of course, one station switch inevitably fosters at least one other switch in the same market. That is, the losing network must find a new affiliate, which in turn stimulates yet another switch, similar to a row of falling dominos. These multiple flip-flops in affiliation—and the resulting flip-flops in program content—caused much confusion for viewers. In addition, advertisers and media buyers had to make adjustments in their media-buying strategies.

These tales of changes in station affiliation underscore the fact that, except for a handful of network owned-and-operated stations, the relationship between a television station and a television network is purely contractual and consequently subject to all kinds of legal entanglements involving programming obligations, compensation fees, commercial adjacencies, and affiliation renewals. Over the years, the duration of most network affiliation contracts has ranged from three to ten years. The original station affiliation business model was a long and reasonably happy marriage until the mid 1990s, when things began to unravel.

The Relationship Today

The first signs of trouble in paradise occurred when network production costs and sports licensing fees (such as NFL football and the Olympics) began to skyrocket out of control. Concurrently, the networks—for the first time—began to lose substantial audiences to cable. These factors, coupled with a lingering recession and shrinking advertising budgets, caused the networks to reevaluate the very core of their decades-old affiliation model. Without getting immersed in esoteric financial details, the bottom-line posture of the networks was that while they were getting ever more in debt, their affiliated stations were earning colossal profits. A common joke about the television station business was that the FCC license was a "license to print money." The proposed solution, in broad terms, was that the affiliated stations must provide not only distribution for network programs but also share some of the costs of doing business. This sharing of the burden could be manifested in several ways, and over the next five years or so, each network hammered out its own plan for the future. Several strategies emerged, including the following:

1   A dramatic decrease in or outright elimination of cash compensation to stations.

2   The introduction of so-called "reverse compensation" schemes in which the station actually pays the network a fee.

3   A reduction or "give-back" of local avails (or adjacencies) in certain network programs or dayparts, enabling the network to acquire more commercial revenue.

4   Insisting on long-term affiliation renewals (typically ten years), in effect squelching any temptation to "shop around" for a more agreeable network parent.

5   Instituting severe penalties for program preemptions by affiliate stations.

6   Insisting on having the right to repurpose programming to cable.

7   Forcing stations to broadcast promos for cable networks owned by the parent network. This is called *cross-promotion*.

The last three items need further explanation. First, program preemptions by affiliates make network executives very unhappy. After all, national advertisers buy expensive network commercials based on the assumption that a message will be seen nationwide. Imagine the distress when a network sales representative must notify an advertising agency that, due to station preemptions, the client's commercial will not be seen in several important cities. In these situations, the agency will typically demand a cash rebate or free commercials in other programs, known as make-goods. Years ago, stations would preempt poorly performing network programs in favor of a syndicated special or movie that provided more local commercial opportunities. In recent years, however, the networks have negotiated tougher affiliation agreements that specify the maximum number of times a station may preempt network programming beyond urgent breaking news stories or weather alerts. Many legal scholars maintain that these strict contracts are unenforceable because the licensed station is legally responsible for all programming, whether the content is obtained from a program syndicator or a network. Therefore, in terms of its FCC license, the station has every legal right not to accept programming from a network. In theory, this mandate should supersede any contractual agreement a station may have with its parent network.

Another area of special concern in recent years has been cable repurposing, in which a broadcast network schedules reruns of a popular program on a cable network owned by the network's parent company. For example, a fresh episode of "Law and Order" first will air on NBC, and then, in two weeks or less, the same episode will air again on TNT cable. All the major television networks have full or partial ownership of prominent cable networks. For example, the Walt Disney Company, which owns the ABC television network, has equity investments in ESPN, Lifetime, and A&E. Similarly, NBC Universal, which owns the NBC television network, has equity in MSNBC, USA, the Sci Fi Channel, and Bravo. Viacom CBS, in addition to its interests in CBS broadcasting, has holdings in MTV networks, which include such popular cable offerings as MTV, Nickelodeon, the Comedy Channel, and Nick at Nite. (CBS and Viacom have since split into two companies.) By repurposing program content onto these owned cable outlets, the broadcast networks can offset some of their programming costs and acquire additional opportunities for selling commercial time.

Related to the repurposing issue is the insertion of promotional announcements (promos) intended to attract audiences to network-owned cable networks. For example, at the conclusion of NBC Nightly News, the network will often insert a promo for an upcoming program airing on MSNBC cable.

Station affiliates have been furious with these practices, because they allegedly push audiences (and ratings) to cable. The parent corporations, however, see a broader picture, in which their owned cable networks are regarded as important business assets in need of quality programming and cross-promotion. Transplanting a popular program from a broadcast network to an "in-house" cable network is seen by some as a smart business strategy. Others, namely broadcast station affiliates, see repurposing and cross-promotion as a betrayal of the relationship. For example, while the ABC network may lose audiences to ESPN, the Walt Disney Company is not particularly upset, as long as the dislodged audiences remain in the corporate "family." Meanwhile, the ABC broadcast affiliates are left trying to attract new audiences.

Looking at all seven items in our prior list, we can see one common theme: the networks' strong-arming their affiliated stations to make concession after concession.

One obvious symptom of the growing tension between stations and networks was the major networks' dropping their membership in the NAB. The networks accused the trade organization of siding too often with local stations on controversial issues. For example, when the networks wanted to raise the limit on network ownership of stations, the NAB publicly criticized the proposal, informing the FCC that proposal threatened the sanctity of local broadcasting. Over the next year or so, most of the broadcast networks dropped their memberships as a gesture of defiance. (Recently the NAB has cajoled most networks to return to the fold). In addition to complaining to their respective networks, affiliated stations from all the major networks have formed the National Association of Network Affiliates (NASA) to represent their interests before the FCC.

Not surprisingly, the stations have capitulated to the networks because the stations want the programming, the theory being that the only thing worse than being under the thumb of your network is to have no network at all. In addition to the economic wrangling, another factor that cannot be ignored by stations is the technology of networking.

Looking Forward

Anticipating the move from analog to digital broadcasting and, in particular, multicasting, all the major television networks have approached their affiliated stations with novel proposals for using their digital subchannels as vehicles for new national niche networks. These include ideas for twenty-four-hour movie channels and news offerings. The individual stations would be offered some type of network compensation and opportunities for advertising. While on paper these proposals may seem attractive, a major roadblock has been the reluctance of the cable industry to retransmit unequivocally this programming without some type of compensation. To date, despite the pleadings by the NAB for required carriage of all digital channels, the FCC has sided with the cable industry's position that these added broadcast networks should compete for distribution on cable, just like any other network. Obviously, this hampers any attempts at quickly creating any new national networks. First, the network would need compliance from two hundred or more affiliated stations. Then, dozens of cable companies would have to be approached to negotiate retransmission agreements. In both instances, the network probably would be compelled to pay a substantial fee to these distributors. With the networks already complaining about runaway operating costs, the specter of paying out more money to establish new mini-networks may be out of the question.

New technology has aggravated the once-stable station-network relationship. As mentioned earlier, during the early years of broadcasting the only means of networking programs to the whole county was through individual over-the-air stations. Today, with over 87 percent of U.S. households subscribing to cable or satellite services, the notion of over-the-air television is in some ways a myth. Most stations could turn off their transmitters with little disruption to audiences or advertisers. Of course, this stunt would be illegal, but nonetheless the circumstances under which people receive television signals exclusively through antennas are just about nonexistent. Traditional television, with its tall transmission towers radiating program content through the airwaves to communities, is essentially obsolete. As a result, television broadcasters are dependent on cable and satellite companies for survival. Acknowledging this vital dependency, the FCC and Congress have enacted laws that protect broadcasters to some degree from being denied access to the viewing public.

For instance, cable operators must carry all local television stations or enter into a retransmission consent agreement, wherein both parties negotiate some type of mutual compensation.

Just because local television stations and their parent networks are dependent on cable and satellite delivery systems does not mean that this is a simple, one-way street. As alluded to in earlier chapters, despite the hundreds of channels made available to subscribers, approximately half of all television viewing occurs among the Big Four networks (ABC, CBS, NBC, and Fox). As a result, we can see that these subscriber-based industries are heavily dependent on the traditional broadcast networks for popular program content. (Imagine the outrage among cable subscribers if a cable franchise did not carry the Super Bowl airing on a broadcast network!) Recognizing this mutual dependence enables the student of media to better understand the industry system, but we need to be aware of another technology-based factor that is often overlooked.

Audiences don't watch technology, they watch programs. Whether the distribution platform is over-the-air, cable, satellite or a computer, the ordinary viewer really does not care a great deal how an episode of "Law and Order" is presented on a screen. In recent years, the television networks have pondered this media fact of life and have begun to have second thoughts about the sacredness of the conventional station affiliation business model.

A Vision of the Future?

For over a half century, the only means by which broadcast networks have distributed programming to audiences has been through their local station affiliates. Furthermore, in order to get this programming distributed on cable and now satellite, the final transaction for these clearances had to include signals originating at local stations. One important exception has been the WB network, which was forced to find an alternative means of acquiring cable distribution that may serve as a vision of the future for the entire industry. The creation of the new CW network, of which the "W" stands for Warner Brothers, has temporarily destabilized this model, but the underlying concept of using cable to distribute exclusively "broadcast" content is still valid.

Because so many small markets do not have a sufficient number of licensed stations to accommodate six national networks, the late-arriving WB network initiated some unique partnerships with local cable systems in the markets ranked 100 and smaller. In simple terms, in exchange for advertising opportunities (commercial avails) on the network, the cable system provided an exclusive channel for WB. Because there was no conventional over-the-air WB broadcast network affiliate in these markets, the presentation of WB programming was, for all intents and purposes, identical to that of a regular cable network. The program content was captured by means of a satellite downlink and then distributed through wires to subscriber homes. The fact that in many of these markets the partnering cable systems were owned by Warner Brothers Cable made the negotiations fairly easy.

As the saying goes, "necessity is the mother of invention," and in this circumstance it was necessary for WB to invent a new business model for distributing its network programming to dozens of small markets throughout the country. By using local cable systems as the primary provider—rather than a conventional over-the-air television station affiliate—the WB network opened the door to possible future deals involving other broadcast networks. No doubt, the new WC network will take advantage of this model in some small markets.

Remember, no law prohibits the broadcast networks from altering their distribution "platform" from broadcast station affiliation to cable. As noted earlier, the television networks are already heavily involved with cable programming. Is repurposing merely one step away from shifting all programming to cable in the future? That is, could a broadcast network simply abandon all its station affiliates and become essentially a cable network like A&E, MTV, or ESPN? Furthermore, could the notion of multicasting, using local-station digital channels, be abandoned in favor of merely persuading cable services to carry these new network offerings as cable networks? Admittedly, about 15 percent of U.S. households do not subscribe either to cable or satellite, but are these the avid and affluent television viewers that programmers and advertisers care about? Looking into the future, as broadband Internet access becomes more prevalent, *video streaming* may someday displace both conventional broadcasting and cable. (Recall that new digital television screens are essentially computer screens.)

Most industry observers believe that as long as the networks maintain their cash-rich, owned-and-operated television stations, attracting substantial local advertising dollars, this network-station breakup is unlikely to occur at least in the near future. But even as a hypothetical scenario, observers of the television industry should understand that this business model, wherein the conventional "broadcast" networks bypass stations, is at least feasible.

For over a half century, local radio and television stations were the only means of exposing network commercials to a nationwide audience at the same moment in time, but with the introduction of alternative technologies, this dependence on stations is not as absolute. Local station operators are more than aware of this tenuous situation. Over the past dozen years, when the affiliates have seemed agitated and restless, network executives have made speeches with veiled threats about "alternative platforms" for program distribution. This saber rattling from the networks, along with growing competition from cable and satellite, has prompted local station operators to invest heavily in local news, the one area where the national networks—either broadcast or cable—cannot compete with local stations. Most media experts see the station-network relationship remaining intact for some time but fraught with tension and squabbles, similar to many long-standing marriages.

Questions for Further Thought

1 Pretend you represent a new television network looking for station affiliates. What strategies might you try to persuade a station to switch affiliations?

2 If you were the general manager of a television station recently "orphaned" by the new consolidated CW network, what programming strategies would you try to fill prime time hours?

3 How do the current issues surrounding the station-network relationship serve as a microcosm for issues facing the television industry as a whole?

4 Looking at what has transpired over the past decade, what do you predict the network-station relationship will be like ten years from now?

Extinction
or Evolution?

The Future of Conventional
Television

At the very beginning of this book we used the metaphor of dismantling a wind-up clock to better understand what made the clock tick. Today's solid-state, digital clocks produce more of a tiny hum than a conspicuous tick-tock, but the principle remains the same. Studying just the individual parts of a system results in only a partial understanding of them. The important insights come when we look at relationships among these parts. Similarly, many of the individual parts found within the television industry have changed greatly since their inception decades ago. The current transition from analog to digital transmission echoes the change from wind-up to electronically powered clocks. The mechanisms for both have changed dramatically over time, but their intended purpose remains constant. Clocks tell time. Television entertains and informs. While looking at the television industry's many parts chapter by chapter, we also tried to maintain a sense of context, or "The Big Picture," of how these parts relate to one another in a complex system. This tactic and some of the jargon has begun to emerge in both academic and professional circles. A recent article in the business section of the *New York Times* referred to " . . . the complex ecosystem of television."[1] For convenience and clarity, we set out to use technology, economics, and regulation as three recurring navigation guideposts for examining the inner workings of the television industry.

In order not to be overwhelmed by the true complexity of the subject, specific chapter topics were extracted from the larger system. While much of the book has so far looked at the television industry today and some of its historical roots, our final chapter takes a brief look at the future.

In the mid-1990s, many crystal-ball gazers predicted that with the explosion in multi-channel services, such as cable, satellite, and the Internet, things would only get worse for the beleaguered television networks and their stations. One of the more pessimistic pundits, Adam Thierer, of the Heritage Foundation, a conservative think-tank, predicted "the death knell for the broadcast networks" and claimed that the introduction of so much viewer choice was "a signal to the world that the old media empires are modern-day dinosaurs headed for extinction."[2] This bleak Darwinian view has proven to be somewhat exaggerated, as have some predictions about the impact of new technologies on the business of television. Back in 2000, a headline on the front cover of the *New York Times Magazine* exclaimed, "The End of the Mass Market. How a New Television Technology Could Destroy Advertising as We Know It."[3] The new device was TiVo, and now, years later, despite warnings that the sky is falling, advertisers continue to spend billions of dollars on television.

Instead of conceding defeat, many savvy media companies have taken inspiration rather than resignation from the notion of technological evolution and are adapting to their new surroundings. They are developing business strategies that will allow them to survive and prosper in the turbulent years to come. Some strategies involve exploiting new technologies, such as digital multicasting and Internet portals. Other strategies involve restructuring old business models, such as duopolies and cable partnerships. Still other survival strategies involve the adoption of brand marketing principles to attract and hold audiences. This does not mean that the future is all blue sky and roses. The system of American television will endure some pain and anxiety, but extinction seems unlikely.

The following are some pivotal challenges the industry will face in coming years. As with so many topics presented in this book, their boundaries are quite porous, inviting interactions with all kinds of surrounding systems.

Coping with New Technologies

One of the more telling pieces of evidence to address the impact of technology on television was an announcement made in 2005 by the

National Academy of Television Arts and Sciences, creating a new category for its renowned annual Emmy Awards. The new entry is titled "Outstanding content distributed via nontraditional delivery platforms."[4] The obvious message here is that television is not what it used to be. Today 87 percent of all U.S. households subscribe either to a cable or satellite service, meaning that only a tiny fraction of the nation truly receives television "over the air." Each year, as the interdependent forces of technology, economics, and regulation shape the industry, the conventional definition of television as a free, advertiser-supported, broadcast service has become almost obsolete, at least from the perspective of *distributing* program content to audiences. After having adapted to the distribution of programming to households by cable and satellite, the television industry is again on the brink of another dramatic transformation. This time the buzzwords are "convergence" and "portability." At a recent consumer electronics show, hardware manufacturers demonstrated a range of non-traditional devices for viewing "television," from cell phones to portable video players to computers with digital-video-recording (DVR) capability. Internet companies, not set-makers, grabbed most of the headlines with various video-on-demand deals in which network programming can be purchased for downloading onto all kinds of devices.

Clearly, the broadcast networks are embracing convergence as a means of staying in business. What is unclear is the role broadcast *stations* will play in this new era, particularly in regard to mobile viewing. These new mobile viewing devices all have a common thread: they *don't rely on the broadcast spectrum*. Instead, most of the broadcast networks' new video services aimed at computers or hand-held devices are delivered through the Internet, typically through cable, wired telephone, or wireless cell-phone networks. Furthermore, the broadcast networks do not appear eager to share this new source of revenue with their station affiliates. The notion of mobile, hand-held reception of over-the-air digital television from individual stations is fraught with problems that will take years to iron out. As one industry observer attending the electronics show put it, "The broadcasters are definitely getting squeezed,"[5] especially station operators. Earlier we examined the often-rocky relationship between stations and networks, and this tension will not lessen as new technologies enable networks to distribute their programming through *non-broadcast means*. Ironically, the one thing that seems to keep the networks from bolting altogether is the fact that they own television stations. To date, these O&Os are highly profitable, especially those licensed to big cities. In fact, several networks have sold off some of their smaller stations in order to purchase new properties in larger markets. Furthermore, the networks like the idea of duopolies, in which one company can own two stations in the same market. Right now, the best example of this is the acquisition by NBC of several Telemundo stations in major cities, creating essentially dual O&Os in the same market. As long as these stations continue to produce handsome profits, their parent networks will probably not abandon the traditional broadcast network model. However, this posture will not halt the networks' investment in other distribution platforms, such as DVDs, plus cable and web-based downloading partnerships. The local affiliated stations not owned by the networks are apparently on their own, although we can see hints that networks might become more ingratiating, specifically in the area of digital multicasting. As discussed in prior chapters, the networks would like to create secondary networks using the new digital sub-channels available to stations. Even though the technology is available to accomplish this today, the regulatory and economic obstacles to the cable industry of carrying these new channels are daunting. It's all about competition.

Coping with Competition

Addressing new technologies inevitably brings us to a discussion of competition. The term had far more clarity when television networks and their allied stations merely competed against each other, but, with the advent of cable, satellite, the Internet, and other technologies, the sources of real competition have increased greatly. For over three decades a three-network oligopoly of ABC, CBS, and NBC dominated the television industry and audience viewing habits. By the mid 1980s, the competitive picture began to change when Fox became a legitimate network player. Later UPN and WB would make things more interesting, but the biggest competition for audiences and advertisers has come from the enormous growth of cable and satellite services. So far, conventional television has managed to survive by providing popular program content that proportionately delivers to advertisers much bigger audiences at one point in time than any cable network. In truth, this advantage is not a function of technology but rather of sound programming and marketing strategies.

Understanding competition properly requires an appreciation of the economic complexities of media today. As discussed earlier in this book, the parent companies of the major broadcast networks are heavily invested in "competing" media. Just as General Motors owns Chevy, Buick, and Cadillac, which "compete" against each other, so Disney owns both ABC and ESPN, which at times compete head-to-head with other with sports programming. Add repurposing of television network content to cable, satellite, and Internet venues, and the concept of competition becomes more complex. For instance, for Disney management, in terms of bottom-line accounting, ESPN is not necessarily competition for ABC, but for

ABC affiliates (that is, stations not owned by the network), ESPN is indeed a genuine competitor for ratings and revenue. Consequently, we can understand how annual network affiliate meetings are often a weird combination of collegiality and consternation. These days, whenever a network has a hit program, the network brass first congratulate the affiliates for their contributions and then repurpose episodes to cable, thus taking the affiliate station representatives on an emotional rollercoaster. This awkward marriage leads to speculation about the future of the television business model in general.

Coping with New Business Models

For over a half century now, the television business model has been grounded in the assumption that audiences would tolerate periodic interruptions in programming for commercial messages purchased by advertisers. A second important assumption has been that audiences would be reasonably attentive to these messages and that, over repeated exposures, a significant number of audience members would actually respond to these messages. Of course, the media are not responsible for marketing the actual product and the creation of a persuasive message, but advertisers assume that somebody was there to see not only the program but also the *inserted commercials*. Research indicates that since the introduction of electronic devices such as remote controls and DVRs, audiences are "zapping" commercial matter at alarming rates. One result has been the rapid growth of product placement tactics as a short-term solution, but does the television industry need to begin looking at alternative models based on the notions of *subscription* and *pay-per-view*? The $1.99 downloading of commercial-free, prime time programs to home computers and portable iPods is the first sign of the industry experimenting with new models. Perhaps the future will be more of a hybrid configuration in which conventional advertiser-supported programming will still exist on a first-run, free basis, but the program's next airing would be made available commercial-free for a nominal fee on a variety of media platforms. In theory, both networks and individual stations could participate in this type of venture.

Coping with Audience Behavior

Of course, a discussion of competition and business models cannot ignore the fact that networks and stations compete for audiences and that ordinary people are experiencing the same media convulsions as the people working in business. Given the ability to record, fast-forward, zap, time-shift, and download content, how will audience behavior change in coming years? One psychological factor that has important implications is that overly abundant choice is not necessarily what people want. Brand researchers are finding that providing consumers with limitless options can reach a point of diminishing returns, in which the "overloaded" human mind desperately seeks ways to reduce the number of realistic choices and simplify decision-making. Most people do not want to deal with two hundred choices of *anything*. The result has been that the number of channels actually viewed regularly is disappointingly small. Several studies conducted by Nielsen and other research companies indicate that for an average American household, there is a viewing threshold of approximately a dozen or so heavily viewed channels. Even in homes where two hundred or more channels are available, the number actually viewed is less than twenty. Several media researchers have adopted the concept of *channel repertoire* to describe this limited array of channels from which audiences select programming. Although repertoires can vary dramatically among audience members, the good news for conventional broadcasters is that the major television networks are still included in almost all of these elite groupings.

We sometimes forget that, despite the massive increase in program options, a day is still only twenty-four hours long. Researchers have found that over the past dozen years, while the amount of program choice has risen dramatically, there has been no substantial increase in the amount of time people spend watching television. Nielsen Media Research reports that for the past twenty years, the amount of time per household dedicated to television viewing has remained almost unchanged; the one exception has been households with digital video recorders, such as TiVo.[6] The disturbing implications for the media companies is that while the number of slices in the programming pie has increased, the overall size of the pie itself has not changed. In other words, more choice has not translated into more viewing. Using brand-marketing terminology, television viewing appears to have evolved into a *mature* or *zero sum* market, where the number of available customers for a product category is relatively stagnant. Therefore, as more brands enter the marketplace, the only means of survival is to take customers (audiences) away from competing brands.

In this same vein, some media observers envision a digital future of what has been coined media "cannibalism," in which multicasting will not necessarily attract new audiences but merely consume existing audiences in different ways. That is, stations run the risk of unintentionally diverting audiences from their primary channel to an array of smaller, digital sub-channels. The burning question for the station operators is: will *advertisers* pay more for reaching these narrower audience segments? If the answer is no, multicasting will become a mere audience trade-off rather than a source of new revenue. Broadcasters will become cannibals, essentially "feeding" off their existing audiences for financial sustenance. One example might be local news. By repeating newscasts or generating updated weather forecasts on digital sub-channels, will stations lose substantial audiences for their flagship newscasts airing on their primary channel? This audience fragmentation leads us logically to a closer look at the future of niche marketing.

Coping with the Niche

More choice leads to more specialized program content. Technological breakthroughs, such as digital compression and fiber optics, are stimulating cable and satellite companies to increase channel capacity even more, and no doubt, the number of niche program formats and the resulting degree of audience fragmentation will grow in coming years. As mentioned in prior chapters, niche theory is about competition and coexistence in highly competitive media markets. Rather than competing head-to-head with all brands within a product category, niches are created that allow the brand to sidestep direct confrontation. This is fine as long as a business is willing to remain relatively small, but most businesses want to grow, and therein rests the challenge for conventional television. In a zero sum marketplace, regardless of the distribution technology, television stations and networks must perform a balancing act of catering to the targeted needs of advertisers without succumbing to the perils of becoming too small. Perhaps the old concept of a gigantic, "mass audience" is indeed obsolete, but savvy media professionals also know that people within a society are more alike than they are different, and as a result, satisfying common needs and desires is still possible. Ted Koppel, of ABC Nightline fame, questions the wisdom of conventional television obsessing over demographically narrow audiences.

> Reaching across the entire spectrum of American television viewers is precisely the broadcast networks' greatest strength. By focusing only on key demographics, by choosing to ignore their total viewership, they have surrendered their greatest advantage.[7]

Coping with Content

The original intention of this book was to take a concise look at the business of television and not to become embroiled in the seemingly endless debates over the societal and cultural impact of television. But even taking a purely business perspective, one must recognize that the creation of program content is essential for the well-being of the system. After all, people don't watch "delivery platforms"; they watch programs, and the future of the television industry ultimately rests on content. The fact that a prime time program might be viewed commercial-free at anytime, in any place does not mean that the audience wants to view the program! More than ever, the creation and marketing of superior program *content* will be how conventional television will differentiate itself from its many competitors.

As described earlier, stations will soon have the option to broadcast in wide-screen, high definition (HDTV). Will the mere enhanced picture quality of television attract audiences, or will the novelty quickly wear off, forcing program producers to focus more on substance than visual packaging? Recall the introduction and evolution of color television. At first, people watched color programs because they were indeed in color but, within a few years, as all programs shifted to color production, audiences became more demanding, and programs produced "in living color" were no longer guaranteed high ratings. HDTV will probably experience the same syndrome of initial popularity followed by pervasive apathy, in which high definition is simply taken for granted.

An alternative to HDTV will be several multicast standard-size digital channels (SDTV). At present, only a handful of stations are offering multicast programming, primarily twenty-four-hour local weather channels and repeat airings of regular newscasts. Because of so few offerings and the reluctance of most cable systems to automatically carry these added channels, the future of providing content through multicasting remains a question mark.

Acknowledging that competition certainly will not go away, many television executives have embraced a management perspective in which networks, stations, and programs are regarded as consumer brands. Cecile Frot-Coutaz, producer of the enormously popular reality program "American Idol," insists that "we don't look at shows purely as television programs. We look at the shows as brands."[8] Today, the media trade press is filled with references to "brand identity," "brand image," "brand extension," and "brand equity." Effective brand management helps to reinforce consumer loyalty, attract new customers, and insulate a product from competitive attack. The real question for the future is: How do we define a media brand in the age of convergence? We are just beginning to see that media content can be consumed in a variety of ways. Technology can no longer be an integral part of a brand identity. David Westen of the Associated Press summarized this attitude for news organizations by stating that "The focus is content, because a good story is a good story, whether it ends up in print, radio, TV or streaming video."[9] Conventional over-the-air television broadcasters must recognize this new environment and learn to change.

Coping with the Role of Government

The dramatic changes in the television industry brought about primarily by new technologies have rekindled debates about the role of government in guiding the future of telecommunications. Arguments for deregulation are louder than ever, with members of the FCC rethinking their own agency's purpose in life. Throughout the commission's history, the interwoven themes of competition and concentration have been the driving forces behind much rule-making, but today, with so much choice available from so many companies, some media observers assert that most FCC deliberations simply miss the point. For example, the highly publicized debate over television station ownership restrictions seems to obscure discussions of far more threatening issues of media dominance brought on by Internet giants such as Yahoo and Google. Professor of media ethics Edward Wasserman warns that "Technological advances have moved us way beyond quaint issues of how many obsolescent TV stations one company should own."[10] The rather glib reference to "obsolescent TV stations" is disturbing. Is conventional television destined for extinction?

Coping with Change

Borrowing from biology and the study of ecosystems, we can see that systems in nature change over time so that an observer of a particular environment may find that, years later, it has become barely recognizable, filled with altered or new species. And yet the overall system is still alive and thriving. Similarly, business systems change over time, sometimes accelerating, sometimes slowing down, sometimes changing direction, but not necessarily falling apart. The system of American television is undergoing an historic transformation in which myriad technological, economic, and regulatory factors are about to converge. In some cases these encounters will be comfortable transitions; in others they will be abrupt collisions. But in the end, this author predicts that the overall system will adapt and prosper. Perhaps our biggest obstacle to understanding is semantics. That is, if in the future audiences no longer receive network or station content directly over the air but rather indirectly through cable, satellite, the Internet, or some other delivery platform, will we still call it television?

Questions for Further Thought

1 Having read this book and particularly this final chapter, what are your predictions about the future of the television industry systems in terms of coping with

- New technologies

- New competition

- New business models

- Niche marketing

- The role of government

- Content

- The whole notion of change

Shop Talk

account executive (AE): A sales person representing a particular television station. The "account" refers to an advertiser in that an AE services advertising accounts that are active on a station.

accrual accounting: An accounting procedure in which expected revenues from sales contracts are reported or accrued as income found in an "accounts receivable" ledger. Because the advertiser does not receive an invoice until after the commercial has aired, the station essentially offers its clients short-term credit.

adjacencies: A local commercial opportunity (see *avails*) placed within or "adjacent" to network programming.

affidavit (also affidavit of performance): A notarized record of commercial announcements provided to advertisers indicating the precise date and time a specific commercial aired. Typically, affidavits are attached to station invoices sent to advertisers (see *station log*).

affiliate: A local station that broadcasts programs provided by an affiliated network. This is a contractual agreement, and stations have been known to network affiliations. Although some affiliates are owned by the networks (see *O and O*), the majority of stations in the United States are independently owned.

analog: Conventional over-the-air television A method of data storage and transmission by wave-like electromagnetic signals radiating from an antenna. American television is making an historic transition from analog to *digital* transmission.

aspect ratio: The ratio of width to height in a television picture. A conventional analog television screen has an aspect ratio of 3 x 4. New high-definition television (HDTV) offers an aspect ratio of 16 x 9, similar to a movie theater screen.

audience turnover (T/O): A measurement of the degree to which the audience of a radio or television program changes over a period of time; specifically, the ratio of cumulative audience over average-quarter-hour audience.

avails: Sales opportunities to insert commercials within a television program break structure. Typically one break will contain several avails that can accommodate commercials of varying lengths (e.g., sixty, thirty, and fifteen seconds).

average-quarter-hour (AQH): Rating measurement used to estimate the size of a station's audience during any fifteen-minute period. Most Nielsen ratings are expressed in average-quarter-hour units.

bandwidth: The amount of information that can be transmitted over a computer network at a given time. The higher the bandwidth, the more data can pass over the network.

barter syndication: The selling of the program broadcast rights to individual stations on a market-by-market basis in which a portion of the commercial opportunities (see *avails*) are withheld or *bartered* by the syndicator to sell to national advertisers.

block programming: A television program-scheduling strategy in which the station or network airs a group or *block* of highly similar programming over extended hours, such as an entire evening of sitcoms.

branding: The art and science of marketing a program, a station, or a network as unique from its competition. The power of a brand name to influence audience attitudes and behavior.

broadcasting: Over-the-air transmission of program content by an FCC-licensed station. Note that cable systems can acquire a broadcast signal off air and then *retransmit* it by wire to subscriber households.

cable penetration (satellite penetration): The percentage of homes within a specified geographical area that subscribe to cable television or satellite.

call letters: Assigned station identification generally beginning with W (east of the Mississippi) and K (west).

cash flow: Operating profit before taxes, depreciation, and interest are subtracted.

census: A research term meaning that every person or household within a designated population, such as a city or county, was contacted for a survey. A survey technique in which a representative sample is not used, and therefore exhibits no sampling error. For most mass-communication research, such as ratings surveys, a true census is impractical.

channel: The assigned broadcast frequency (UHF or VHF) of a television station. Today, all stations have been assigned an additional *digital channel*, which eventually will replace their older *analog channels*. See also *simulcast*.

channel capacity (cable capacity): In cable, the number of channels that can be carried on a given system. Not to be confused with over-the-air television broadcast channels, which are limited and regulated by the FCC. The cable industry claims that it cannot automatically *retransmit* additional digital *multicast channels* from television stations because of a lack of channel capacity.

chilling effect: The influence of government threats and intimidation on journalists pursuing a controversial story. Essentially the motivations to report the story are "chilled" by fear of some kind of reprisal, such as jail time for contempt. Many First Amendment Supreme Court rulings have used this term in defending the freedom of the press.

city of license: The FCC-designated city in which a television station must place its primary studios and nearby transmitting tower.

clearance: The procedure in which a network-affiliated station formally agrees to air a particular program. A station essentially "clears the way" for the network to reach a desired audience. See also *affiliate*.

clutter: An excessive number of commercials within a program. Advertisers worry that clutter may reduce the effectiveness of their commercials. Programmers worry that clutter causes audiences to change channels.

commercial: A paid advertising announcement or "spot."

commercial speech: A type of expression, mostly in commercials and other forms of advertising, protected to a limited degree by the First Amendment to the U.S. Constitution.

composite video signal: The final, electronically assembled television picture that an audience actually sees on a television screen.

convergence: The bringing together through digital technology of various media platforms, such as print, broadcast, and Internet, into a common computer-based environment.

cost per point (CPP): A commercial unit cost based on comparing the total cost of a commercial with the number of household or demographic rating points delivered by a program. An estimate of how much it costs an advertiser to reach one rating point (or 1 percent of the market).

cost per thousand (CPM): A commercial unit cost based on comparing the total cost of a commercial with the number of households or demographic members (expressed in thousands) delivered by a program. An estimate of how much it costs an advertiser to reach 1,000 units of its target audience.

counter-programming: A television programming strategy in which a station or network schedules program content that is perceived as opposite to that offered by a competing station or network. For example, a network may schedule a female-oriented ice skating special against NFL football.

coverage contour: A visual presentation or map of where a television station's signal can be received adequately by a regular television set. The actual contour represents the connections among furthest geographical reception points.

cross-promotion: A marketing strategy in which different media owned by the same parent company promote each other. An example would be a broadcast network airing promos for one of its owned cable networks.

deficit financing: A program-production strategy in which a network agrees to pay a producer for only a portion of the production costs of a pilot or the first few episodes of an untested program. The program producer operates temporarily in a "deficit" posture, hoping that the new venture will eventually become a hit so that he or she can recoup these losses.

demographics: Statistical data pertaining to audience age, sex, race, income, education, marital status, and other quantifiable descriptions. Nielsen ratings provide some demographic information.

deregulation: The political trend to have less government involvement in the business of broadcasting. In recent years, many media rules and regulations have been abandoned in favor of a free-market approach to the conduct of business.

designated market area (DMA): A Nielsen Media Research term for a group of counties in which a television station obtains the greatest portion of its audience. Each U.S. county is part of only one DMA. A more detailed description of a television *market*. See also *city of license*.

digital television (DTV): The next generation in television transmission, intended to replace analog television by 2009. DTV offers high-resolution pictures and sound using computer protocols rather than electromagnetic waves.

digital video recorders (DVRs): Television program recording devices, such as the popular TiVo, that allow audiences to stop, start, reverse, and fast-forward program content, including the avoidance or *zapping* of commercials.

downlink (uplink): An outside dish antenna that receives signals from a satellite. Almost all television stations and cable systems use downlinks to receive program content from networks and syndicators. Conversely, a dish antenna that sends signals up to a satellite is called an *uplink*.

duopoly: Ownership by the same company of two television stations operating in the same market. The FCC has strict guidelines as to when and how a legal duopoly can exist.

encryption: The process of encoding a television signal. Encryption is used to scramble premium cable channels so that non-subscribers cannot view it. Additionally, station encryption is used in the experimental *portable people meter*, allowing passive identification of stations being viewed by a sample audience.

exclusivity (exclusive rights): A portion of a contractual agreement between a station and a network or a station and a program syndicator in which the station is provided with the exclusive rights within its *Designated Market Area (DMA)* to broadcast certain programs. See also *renewal agreement*.

Federal Communications Commission (FCC): Federal agency created by the Communications Act of 1934 that consists of five commissioners appointed by the president and confirmed by the Senate. The commission regulates television, radio, wire, satellite, and cable in all fifty states and U.S. territories.

fin-syn rules (financial interest and syndication rules): The laws passed by the Federal Communications Commission in the 1970s limiting the networks' ownership and domestic syndication of the programming they broadcast. The regulations were repealed in 1994 because of increased media competition brought on by cable and satellite serv-

ices. The repeal has led to the phenomenon of one network producing programming that appears on another network.

first-run syndicated programming: Syndicated programming intended
to be aired on individual television stations with no prior exposure
on a network. See also *off-network syndication.*

frequency: Media-buying term referring to the average number of times
an audience is exposed to a commercial. Typically, frequency data is
presented simultaneously with audience reach data (i.e., a "reach and
frequency analysis").

futures (future selling): An off-network syndicated program-selling strategy in which the producers of a successful network program encourage station bidding for the future broadcast rights. Winning stations
must often wait several years before the program can actually be aired
on local television.

gross rating points (GRP): A media buying term that represents the sum
of the ratings of all program exposures purchased by an advertiser.
For example, an ad campaign consisting of three commercials in
programs delivering a "10" rating each would generate thirty GRPs.

hammock (hammocking): A program-scheduling strategy in which a station or network schedules a new or poorly performing program
between two strong programs.

HDTV (high-definition television): The new digital replacement to decades-
old analog transmission. HDTV features superior picture resolution
in a wide-screen format similar to a movie theater screen. See also
digital television and *multicasting.*

horizontal sync and vertical sync: An engineering term referring to the
process of synchronizing the horizontal and vertical scanning components of an analog television set.

HUTs and PUTs: Nielsen ratings terminology referring to households using
television (HUT) or persons using television (PUT). The *HUT-level* can
be expressed as a whole number (000) or as a percentage of the total
population under study.

hyphenated market: A television market identified by more than one
FCC city of license, such as Dallas-Ft. Worth or Albany-Schenectady-
Troy.

independent: A television station that has no network affiliation. An
independent must rely on local and syndicated programming.

informed consent: A legal document signed by a person volunteering to
be in a research study, such as a ratings sweep, agreeing that he or

she has been adequately *informed* about the nature of the study and willingly *consents* to participate.

inherited audience (inheritance effects): The portion of the audience of a television program that is acquired ("inherited") from the program scheduled immediately before it. Sometimes referred to as "lead-in effect."

interference (signal interference): The consequence of two or more broadcasting stations operating on the same or nearly the same frequency (or channel). Television sets are unable to differentiate between the overlapping signals, resulting in unacceptable reception for audiences.

inventory: A sales term referring to the total number of commercial opportunities (see *avails*) allotted to a particular program.

license (licensing agreement): The legal authorization by the FCC for an individual or organization to operate a broadcast station. A licensing agreement typically refers to a contract between a station and a program syndicator. See also *syndication* and *exclusivity*.

local marketing agreement (LMA): A business agreement in which one station provides programming and sales support for another station in exchange for shared revenue. For example, many large stations now provide a 10:00 PM newscast to a smaller station in the same market. N.B.: An LMA is not a *duopoly*, in which both stations are actually owned by the same company.

local programming: Programming produced and aired by a local station using its own personnel and facilities. Today most local programming is news.

low power television or LPTV (community television): An FCC designation for a television service consisting of licensed television stations operating at very low power levels. Created in the 1980s, their purpose was to encourage localized community programming that larger, "full power" stations would probably avoid.

make-goods: Free commercials provided to an advertiser because of an on-air technical malfunction or, more commonly, because of disappointing program ratings. The broadcaster essentially "makes good" on a promise to air the commercial properly and deliver a minimum audience rating. See also *projected ratings*.

market: The geographical area served by a radio or television station. See also *designated market area* and *exclusivity*. Also refers to audiences as markets for advertisers, such as the "baby boomer market" or the "working-women market."

multicasting (multiplexing): Taking advantage of digital transmission technology. (Television stations can now broadcast or *multicast* on more than one channel.) A technological trade-off is that, while multicasting, the station cannot broadcast in wide-screen, high definition (HDTV). Instead, these transmissions are in standard digital format, or SDTV.

must-carry rule: FCC regulation requiring that cable systems "must carry" all locally licensed television stations operating within the cable franchise area. This process involves the technical retransmission of the station's over-the-air signal.

National Association of Broadcasters (NAB): The most powerful trade group representing the interests of the radio and television broadcasters. Based in Washington, DC, near the FCC and the Capitol, the NAB is a formidable lobbying organization. As it is primarily concerned with the priorities of local television stations, the major networks have not always been pleased with NAB policies.

National Cable and Telecommunications Association (NCTA): Essentially the cable industry's version of the above-mentioned NAB. An equally powerful trade organization that often battles with the NAB over government regulation of media.

national spot advertising: Commercials purchased on local television stations by national advertisers. Typically a *station rep firm* acts as an intermediary between the station and a national advertising agency or media-buying firm. Rather than advertising nationwide on network television, national spot allows advertisers to select specific geographical markets.

NATPE International: Formerly called the National Association of Television Program Executives, this trade organization concentrates on domestic and international syndicated programming issues and transactions. Recognized primarily for its annual marketplace convention attended by syndicators and station representatives.

network: A media company that provides programming on a contractual basis to a large group of station *affiliates* representing all or nearly all of the 210 markets in the United States. One station per market is given exclusive rights to this programming.

network compensation ("net comp"): By becoming a network affiliate, stations in the past were *compensated* with monthly cash payments in exchange for carrying network programs. In recent years, however, network compensation has been eliminated or reduced substantially. In some cases, the business model has been changed to a "reverse compensation" structure in which the station now pays the network.

network programming: Programs produced and distributed by a network to its affiliated stations.

niche programming: Programming that caters to a narrow audience segment, and an alternative to conventional "mass communication." In general, the cable industry has embraced niche program content more than television broadcasters, who still aim for larger, more diverse audiences.

Nielsen Media Research: The major supplier of television and cable audience ratings in the United States.

nonresponse error: Research terminology referring to the degree to which people are unavailable, unable, or unwilling to participate in a study. Typically expressed as a percentage of the total number of people solicited.

O and O (O&O): An abbreviation for network *owned-and-operated* stations. Although most stations in the United States are independently owned, a substantial number of major-market stations are licensed to the networks. Stations licensed to group owners are sometimes referred to as *group O and Os*.

off-network syndication: Syndicated "rerun" programming intended to be aired on individual television stations after several years of exposure on a major network. Often popular programs are placed into off-network syndication while fresh episodes are still being produced for the networks. Once in syndication, the episodes can be sold to stations affiliated with any network.

opportunistic market: A television sales market in which advertisers essentially wait until the last possible moment to purchase commercials, hoping for an "opportunity" for a discounted rate on unsold commercial *inventory*. See also *upfront market* and *scatter market*.

Overnights: Television ratings available within a day (i.e., "overnight") of broadcast and drawn from sample households in markets provided with Nielsen meters. Overnights are obtained for both national and local markets.

over-the-air-station: A broadcast facility that transmits its signal through the air to receiving devices such as radio and television sets.

people meter: Patented by Nielsen, this device is attached to a home television set and records the television-viewing behavior of sample participants. In order to record demographic information, people are requested to log on to and log off of a viewing room using a remote key pad.

pilot: A television program produced as a prototype of a series being considered for airing on a network. Script approval is typically necessary before a pilot goes into production.

pixels: The electronic "dots" found within a television picture. Each pixel is assigned a color and intensity. Lines of pixels are combined and interpreted by a television set to form a *composite video signal*, which ultimately is what audiences see on their television screens .

portable people meter (PPM): An experimental, portable audience-measurement device being developed by a partnership between Nielsen and the Arbitron Company. The meter, which is about the size of a pager and is worn by survey participants, is capable of recognizing *encrypted* identification codes aired by radio and television stations.

power ratio (power index): A financial calculation used by investors and station managers that compares a station's share of audience with its share of market advertising revenue. In theory, a successful station should earn at least its "fair share" of revenue based on relative audience delivery.

preemption (program and commercial preemptions): A practice used in two distinctly different situations. First, a *program preemption* occurs when a station's management decides not to carry (see *clearance*) a program offered by its affiliated network. Second, a *commercial preemption* occurs when one advertiser is willing to pay more than another for a commercial avail. The losing bidder gets preempted or "bumped" from the schedule. See also *station log* and *traffic department*.

prime time: Generally 8:00 to 11:00 PM except in portions of the Midwest central time zone.

Prime Time Access Rule (PTAR): An FCC ruling instituted in the 1970s to limit the power of the big networks. Network-affiliated stations operating in the top fifty U.S. markets were given "access" to the 7:00–8:00 PM prime time hour, originally programmed by the networks, to broadcast local and syndicated programs.

product placement (product integration): The paid insertion within a television program of various branded props, such as automobiles, cereal boxes, and soda bottles. Advertisers see product placement as an alternative to conventional "spot" advertising.

projected ratings: A sales and media buying term referring to the *predicted* ratings performance of an upcoming program. Commercial rates are often determined by projected ratings. Failure to achieve projected ratings can result in an advertiser receiving free commercials or *make-goods*.

promo: A "commercial" airing on a station or network intended to persuade audiences to watch a particular program. Typically, promos are
scheduled in the same *avail positions* as revenue-producing commercials. Some promos occupy unsold commercial avails, while others
are given guarantees of "fixed" placement within a program. See
cross-promotion.

psychographics: A marketing research term dealing with audience attitudes, behaviors, values, opinions, and beliefs. The notion of "lifestyles"
is often used when discussing psychographics. Used in conjunction
with *demographic* analysis of audiences.

public broadcasting: Noncommercial radio and television stations that are
supported by individual subscribers, foundations, government, and
other funding sources, including corporations. Public Broadcasting
System (PBS) is the most noteworthy noncommercial U.S. television
network service.

public interest (public interest, convenience and necessity): A legal phrase
often used by the FCC to justify its regulation of electronic media such
as radio, television, and cable. The concept maintains that, in return
for using the public airwaves free of charge, broadcasters are obligated to provide programming that is in the "best interests" of the
community. This would typically mean news and public-affairs
programming.

public service announcements (PSAs): Free "commercial" time donated
by radio and television stations to legitimate nonprofit organizations. Most often, PSAs occupy unsold commercial *avails*. See also
promos.

PUT: A Nielsen ratings term for *persons using television* during a specific
time period. The PUT-level can be expressed as a whole number
(000) or as a percentage of the total population under study. See also
HUT.

random sample (probability sample): A research sample in which every
member of the population under study has an equal chance or equal
probability of being selected. A sample that is not random is considered biased. Random samples allow researchers to calculate margins of statistical error. See *sampling error*.

rating (rating points): The size of a television audience expressed as a percentage of the total population under study. For example, a program
that delivers an audience of 10,000 households in a market consisting of 50,000 households generates a 20 rating (i.e., 10,000 is one-
fifth, or 20 percent, of 50,000).

reach: A media-buying term referring to the cumulative number of individuals or households exposed to a program or a commercial. Also

called cume and unduplicated audience. Typically, reach data is presented simultaneously with *frequency* data (i.e., a "reach and frequency analysis").

renewal agreement: The negotiation and re-signing of a contractual agreement between a station and its affiliated network or a station and a program syndicator to maintain the *exclusive broadcast rights* to certain programs. See also *affiliate* and *syndication*.

repurposing: The practice by broadcast networks of scheduling repeat episodes of popular programs on cable. Most often, the designated cable channel is owned by the same parent media company as the television network.

resolution: The technical clarity of a television picture. Digital television is said to provide better picture resolution than conventional analog television.

retransmission: Acquiring a television signal off air by a cable system and then distributing the content to cable subscribers. Retransmission has become a controversial regulatory issue, particularly with the introduction of digital *multicasting* by television stations. See also *channel capacity*.

revenue potential: The calculation of the maximum amount of sales revenue a program could plausibly produce for a station. Critical factors include *projected* ratings, estimates of commercial rates based on ratings, the available commercial *inventory*, and the cost of local production or the cost of syndicated broadcast rights (see *syndication*).

sampling error (margin of error): The calculated reliability of research study results acquired from a random sample. Sample size and the variability of responses contribute to the degree of sampling error. All findings from sample-based research are estimates of what is probably true in the larger population under study. See also *census* and *random sample*.

satellite: A communication device orbiting the earth used to send broadcast and cable program content great distances. Television stations use satellite *downlinks* to acquire program content from networks and syndicators.

scarcity of spectrum: A legal concept used for many years by the FCC to justify the licensing of radio and television station owners. Based on the limited amount of electromagnetic spectrum (i.e., frequencies) that can be made available to potential station operators. With the proliferation of multi-channel cable, satellite, and Internet content providers, the scarcity of spectrum legal argument has become less persuasive. See also *FCC* and *public interest*.

scatter market: A television sales and media-buying term referring to the placement of commercial campaigns by advertisers on a quarterly calendar basis. This serves as an alternative to the *upfront market*, in which advertisers commit media budgets for the entire year. The scatter strategy allows advertisers to make periodic adjustments to their media plans.

share: The size of an audience expressed as a percentage of the households or people actually using television at that time; see *HUTs* and *PUTs*. For example, a program that delivers 10,000 households when 20,000 households are watching (the HUT level) generates a 50 share (10,000 is 50 percent of 20,000).

simulcast: Simultaneous broadcast over two or more stations or simultaneous broadcast through analog and digital transmission by one station.

sponsorships: An alternative to conventional spot commercials in that the advertiser is credited with supporting an entire program or segment of a program. In addition to these special on-air credits, sponsors usually receive some spot commercials within the program. During the early development of radio and television, sponsors often produced the program content.

spots: Commercials; paid announcements. Occasionally *promos* and *PSAs* are also referred to as spots.

station: Broadcast facility given a specific frequency by the FCC.

station identification: On-air disclosure of a station's *call letters* immediately followed by its *channel* number and *city of license*. For example, *WTVJ, Channel 10, Miami.*

station log: Document produced daily containing specific operating information as outlined in FCC rules and regulations. This includes the exact airtimes of all programs and commercials. By law, the station log is available for public inspection. See also *affidavit of performance.*

station rep firm A company acting on behalf of local stations to national advertising agencies. Rep firms negotiate the purchase of *national spot* advertising.

statistical weighting (sample balancing): A common statistical procedure used in sample-based research to compensate for insufficient quantities of certain key demographic groups. This occurs when the demographic composition of an acquired sample does not match that of the population under study. Instead of returning to the field and soliciting more participants, the researcher applies a statistical "weight" to the responses given by available sample members.

stripped programming (stripping) The practice of scheduling the same television program five days or seven days a week at the same time. For example, stations will strip a syndicated game show Monday through Friday at 7:00 PM. The opposite of stripping is checkerboarding, in which a different program airs each night, as can be found in most prime time schedules.

sub-channels: Additional broadcast channels made available to television stations converting to digital transmission. See also *multicasting*.

sweep: A Nielsen ratings term referring to the periodic, four-week-long audience survey periods in which all 210 television markets are measured through the use of paper diaries. All markets have sweeps scheduled for November, February, May, and July. A number of larger markets experience additional sweep months.

syndicated programming (syndication): Television programs sold market-by-market to individual stations; see *first-run* syndication and *off-network* syndication. Through contract negotiations, a station buys the exclusive broadcast rights from the syndicator for that particular market.

system theory: The systematic study of interdependence based on the assumption that the whole of something is more than the sum of its parts. System theory has been called the "science of complexity." The television industry can be studied as a system in which the *relationships* among its components are as important to our understanding as the individual components.

table of allotments: An FCC document outlining the distribution of all television channels, both analog and digital, to their respective *city of license*. Given sufficient geographical separation, channel numbers can be repeated throughout the country.

target audience: A specific demographic audience group that advertisers want to reach with their commercial messages. Because of the demand for certain types of audiences, television stations and networks attempt to attract these target audiences through programming and promotion.

telephone coincidentals: A survey methodology in which audiences are contacted by telephone and asked what they are watching at that moment (i.e., coincidental to answering the phone call). Nielsen uses telephone coincidentals to double-check the reliability of results coming from its metered and diary surveys.

tent-pole (tent-poling): A program-scheduling strategy in which a highly popular program is placed between two less well-performing programs (see also *hammocking*). The theory is that the popular program can act as a bridge to carry audiences through an evening.

traffic: The station or network department responsible for *scheduling* programs, commercials, promos, and public service announcements (PSAs). See *station log*.

UHF (ultra high frequency): The part of the electromagnetic spectrum containing television channels 14 to 69. See also VHF.

upfront market: A sales and media-buying term referring to time of year (typically the late spring and early summer) when the television networks sell to national advertisers the bulk of their prime time *commercial avails* for the entire year. During the hectic upfront selling season, some advertisers commit to over 70 percent of their total media budget. See *scatter market* and *opportunistic market* for alternatives to the upfront market.

upgrading/downgrading: A program-scheduling term referring to changing the day and time when a particular program airs on a station. Upgrading means shifting a program to a more attractive time period, when more people are watching television, such as prime time. Downgrading means shifting to a lesser time period, such as late night. These shifts can influence the *revenue potential* of the program.

v-chip: A computerized device in a television set that automatically blocks receipt of specific programs that are coded to indicate that they contain violence. The v-chip is activated at the option of the viewer.

vertical integration: The process by which a media firm has financial investments in the production, distribution, and exhibition of a product, such as a television program or movie. For example ABC, NBC, and Fox are corporate partners with major production studios.

vertical sync: See *horizontal sync*.

VHF (very high frequency): The part of the electromagnetic spectrum containing television channels 2 to 13. See also UHF.

video-on-demand (VOD): Programming available to an audience at any time or any day. Similar to video rental, but there is no need to go to a retail store. Instead, the transaction is accomplished at home electronically by means of computers, telephone, cable, or satellite technology. So far, VOD programming has been commercial free, but some business entrepreneurs are experimenting with *free* VOD that contans commercials.

wireless access: The ability to access the Internet and download television programming without being hard-wired to a cable or telephone connection.

yield management: An economic term referring to the art and science of maximizing profit from a limited and perishable (time-sensitive) inventory, such as airline seats, hotel rooms, or a station's commercial *inventory*.

zapping: The practice of purposely avoiding commercials by using an electronic device such as a remote control to change channels, or a digital video recorder (DVR) to fast-forward through the commercial break.

Notes

Chapter 1

1   Ludwig von Bertalanffy, *General System Theory: Foundations, Development, Applications* (New York: George Braziller Press, 1999).

2   William G. Covington, Jr., *Systems Theory Applied to Television Station Management in the Competitive Marketplace* (New York: University Press of America, 1997).

3   Marco Iansiti and Roy Levien, "Strategy as Ecology," *Harvard Business Review* 82 (2004): 68–79.

4   Jan LeBlanc Wicks, George Sylvie, C. Ann Hollifield, Stephen Lacy, and Ardyth Broadrick Sohn, *Media Management: A Casebook Approach* (Mahwah, NJ: Lawrence Erlbaum Associates, 2004).

5   Lynn Hirshberg, "Giving Them What They Want," *New York Times Magazine*, 4 September 2005, pp. 30–35.

6   Marshall McLuhan and Quentin Fiore, *The Medium Is the Massage* (New York: Bantam Books, 1967).

Chapter 2

1   Peter Edidin, "Confounding Machines: How the Future Looked," *New York Times*, 28 August 2005, Ideas and Trends section.

2   August E. Grant and Jennifer H. Meadows, *Communication Technology Update*, 9th ed. (Burlington, MA: Focal Press, 2004).

3   Erwin Krasnow, *The Politics of Broadcast Regulation: UHF Television: The Quest for Compatability*, 3rd ed. (New York: St. Martin's Press, 1982).

4   Federal Radio Commission (FRC), *First Annual Report: 1927* (Washington: Government Printing Office, 1927), pp. 10–11.

5   Eric Barnow, *The Golden Web: A History of Broadcasting in the United States Part II* (New York: Oxford University Press, 1970).

6   Federal Communications Commission, "About the FCC: A Consumer Guide to Our Organization, Functions and Procedures," www.fff.gov/aboutus.html (2005).

7   Robert Hilliard and Michael Keith, *The Hidden Screen: Low Power Television in America* (New York: M.E Sharpe, 1999).

8   Community Broadcasters Association, www.dtvnow.org.

9   Christopher Sterling and John Kitross, *Stay Tuned: A History of American Broadcasting*, 3rd ed. (Mahwah, NJ: Lawrence Erlbaum Associates, 2001).

10   Stewart Louis Long, *The Development of the Television Network Oligopoly* (New York: Arno Press, 1979).

11   FCC 1952, Federal Communications Commission Amendment of Section 3.606 of Commission Rules and Regulations (Sixth Report and Order), 41 FCC 148 (1952).

12   "Dissenters Are Jones and Hennok," *Broadcasting and Telecasting*, 17 April 1952, p. 38.

13   Stanley Besen, *Misregulating Television: Network Dominance and the FCC* (Chicago: University of Chicago Press, 1984).

14   Federal Communications Commission Notice of Proposed Rule Making. All-Channel Television Receivers, 18 September 1962.

15   *The DuMont Television Network Historical Website*, http//members.aol.com/cingram/television/dumont.html.

16   Federal Communications Commission Press Release, "Commission Adopts Table of Allotments for DTV," MM Docket No. 87-268 (3 April 1997).

17   Federal Communications Commission, "Digital Television Consumer Facts," www.fcc.gov/cgb/consumerfacts/digitaltv.html.

18   Sylvia Chan-Olmsted and Louisa Ha, "Internet Business Models for Broadcasting: How Television Stations Perceive and Integrate the Internet," *Journal of Broadcasting and Electronic Media* 47 (2003): 197–218.

19   WFLA-TV, www.wfla.com.

20   Michael Wirth, "Issues in Media Convergence," in *Handbook of Media Management and Economics*, ed. Alan Albarran, Sylvia Chan-Olmsted, and Michael Wirth (New York: Lawrence Erlbaum Publishing, 2006).

Chapter 3

1   Paddy Chayevsky quotation taken from *quotegarden.com* website.

2   "Getting There. The first 75 years of Broadcasting." *Broadcasting and Cable*, 125 (November 6, 1995) p 42.

3   Webster, J. G., Phalen, P. F., Lichty, L. W. (2000). *Ratings Analysis: Theory and practice* (Hillsdale, NJ: Lawrence Erlbaum).

4   Alan B. Albarran, *Management of Electronic Media*, 3rd edition (New York: Thompson Wadsworth, 2006).

5   Charles Warner and Joseph Buchman, *Media Selling: Broadcast, Cable, Print and Interactive* (Ames, IO: Iowa State Press- Blackwell Publishing, 2004).

6   Nielsen Media Research website: www. nielsenmediaresearch.com.

7   NATPE website: www.natpe.org.

8   Sterling Quinlan, *Inside ABC: American Broadcasting Company's Rise to Power* (New York: Hastings House, 1979).

9   Daniel M. Kimmel, *The Fourth Network: How Fox Broke the Rules and Reinvented Television* (Chicago: Ivan R, Dee Publishing, 2004).

10 Christopher Sterling and John Kitross, *Stay Tuned: A History of American Broadcasting*, (3rd edition) (Mahwah, NJ: Lawrence Erlbaum Associates, 2001).

11 Alison Alexander, James Owers and Rod Carveth, Anne Hollifield and Albert Greco. *Media Economics: Theory and Practice*, 3rd edition (Mahwah, NJ: Lawrence Erlbaum, 2004**).

12 McDowell, W.S., & Dick, S. J. (2004). "Has lead-in lost its punch? A Comparison of Prime Time Ratings Inheritance Effects Comparing 1992 with 2002." *International Journal of Media Management*, 5, 285-293.

13 Susan Tyler Eastman, Douglas Ferguson, *Broadcast and Cable Programming. Strategies and Practices*, 7th edition (Belmont, CA: Wadsworth, 2005).

14 Susan Tyler Eastman, Douglas A. Ferguson and Robert A. Klein, *Promotion and Marketing for Broadcasting, Cable and the Web* (Boston: Focal Press, 2002).

15 Walter McDowell and Alan Batten, *Branding TV: Principles and Practices* (Washington DC: National Association of Broadcasters and Focal Press, 2005)

16 Steve McClellan, "The Venerable AP is Mulling New Curely Cues," *Broadcasting and Cable*, October 27, 2003, 34.

Chapter 4

1   Milton Berle Quote taken from *quotegarden.com* website.

2   Christopher Sterling and John Kitross, *Stay Tuned: A History of American Broadcasting*, 3rd edition (Mahwah, NJ: Lawrence Erlbaum Associates, 2001).

3   Barbara A. Cherry, "Regulatory and Political Influences on Media Management,"

in *Handbook of Media Management and Economics*. ed. Alan Albarran, Sylvia Chan-Olmsted and Michael Wirth (Mahwah, NJ: Lawrence Erlbaum, 2006).

4   William David Sloan, *Perspectives on Mass Communication History* (Hillsdale, NJ: Lawrence Erlbaum, 1991).

5   Tony Chiu, *CBS The First 50 Years* (New York: Stoddart, 1998).

6   John W. Dimmick, *Media Competition and Coexistence: The Theory of the Niche* (Mahwah, NJ: Lawrence Erlbaum, 2002).

7   Ben Grossman, "Brands Abandoned," *Broadcasting and Cable*, September 12, 2005, 16.

8   Charles Warner and Joseph Buchman, *Media Selling: Broadcast, Cable, Print and Interactive* (Ames, IO: Iowa State Press- Blackwell Publishing, 2004).

9   Television Bureau of Advertising (TVB) website: tvb.org.

10   Shane Fox, *Pricing and Rate Forecasting Using Broadcast Yield Management* (Washington D.C.: National Association of Broadcasters, 1992).

11   Srinivas Bollapragada and Marc Garbiras, "Scheduling Commercials on Broadcast Television," *Operations Research* 52 (2004): 337-345.

12   Sergio Zyman and Armin Brott, *The End of Advertising as We Know It* (New York: Wiley, 2002).

13   Joseph D. Rumbo, "Consumer Resistance to the Amount of Advertising Clutter," *Psychology and Marketing* 19 (2001): 127-148.

Chapter 5

1   Mark Fowler, "A Marketplace Approach to Broadcast Regulation," *Texas Law Review* 60 (1982): 1–51.

2   One of many sources for U.S. documents, including the U.S. Constitution and Bill of Rights, is the U.S. House of Representatives at http://www.house.gov/house/Educate.shtml.

3   Justice Holmes quotation taken from Douglas M. Fraleigh and Joseph S. Tuman, *Freedom of Speech in the Marketplace of Ideas* (Boston: Bedford-St. Martin's, 1997).

4   *New York Times* v. *Sullivan*, 376 U.S. 254 (1964).

5   Radio and Television News Directors Association (RTNDA), http://www.rtnda.org.

6   National Association of Broadcasters (NAB), http://www.nab.org.

7   National Cable and Telecommunications Association (NCTA), http://www.ncta.com.

8   *Webster's College Dictionary* (New York: Barnes and Noble, 2006).

9   An excellent book addressing the complexities of media ethics is Clifford Christians, Kim Rotzoll, Mark Fackler, Kathey Brittain McKee, and Robert Woods, Jr., *Media Ethics: Cases and Moral Reasoning* (Boston: Pearson Publishing, 2005).

10   See http://www.quotationspage.com/quotes/Edward_R._Murrow/.

11 Christopher Sterling and John Kitross, *Stay Tuned: A History of American Broadcasting*, 3rd ed. (Mahwah, NJ: Lawrence Erlbaum Associates, 2001).

12 *Red Lion Broadcasting Co. v. FCC*, 395 U.S. 367 (1969).

13 FCC, http://www.fcc.gov/aboutus.html.

14 Philip Napoli, "The Unique Nature of Communications Regulation: Evidence and Implications for Communication Policy Analysis," *Journal of Broadcasting and Electronic Media* 43 (1999): 565–81.

15 From "Regulatory and Political Influence on Media Management and Regulation," in *Handbook of Media Management and Economics*, ed. Alan Albarran, Sylvia Chan-Olmsted, and Michael Wirth (Mahwah, NJ: Lawrence Erlbaum Publishing, 2006).

Chapter 6

1 Joe Mandese, "Nielsen's Brave New World," *Broadcasting and Cable*, 21 February 2005, p. 26.

2 Jon Gertner, "Watching What You Watch," *New York Times Magazine*, 10 April 2005, p. 34.

3 Nielsen Media Research, www.nielsenmedia.com.

4 For more detailed information see the Arbitron website, www.arbitron.com.

5 James G. Webster, Patricia F. Phalen, and Lawrence W. Lichty, *Ratings Analysis: The Theory and Practice of Audience Research*, 3rd ed. (Mahwah, NJ: Lawrence Erlbaum Associates, 2006).

Chapter 7

1 G. N. Hess, *A History of the DuMont Television Network*. Ph.D Dissertation, Northwestern University, 1960. (Reprinted in book form, 1979 by Arno Press, New York).

2 FCC (1982). Federal Communications Commission. MB Docket 78-391, July 1982. In the matter of improvement to uhf television reception.

3 The following are recommended histories of the DuMont and Fox Networks:

> David Weinstein, *The Forgotten Network: DuMont and the Birth of American Television*. Philadelphia, PA. Temple University Press, 2004)

> Ted Bergman, *The Dumont Television Network: What Happened?: A significant Episode in the History of Broadcasting* (Lanham, MD, Scarecrow Press, 2002).

> Daniel Kimmel, *The Fourth Network: How Fox Broke the Rules and Reinvented Television* (Chicago, IL: Ivan R. Dee Publishing, 2004).

L. Thomas and B. R. Litman, "Fox Broadcasting Company, Why Now? An Economic Study of the Rise of the Fourth Broadcast Network." *Journal of Broadcasting and Electronic Media*, 35 (1991).

Chapter 8

1 Edward Rathburn, "Marketers Take Promax Spotlight," *Broadcasting and Cable*, 12 June 1995, p. 12.

2 A comprehensive list of licensed television stations, their group owners, and network affiliations can be obtained directly from the FCC or from several business reference books, such as the annual *Broadcasting and Cable Yearbook* found in many university libraries.

3 More detailed information about the history and impact of PTAR and Fin-Syn Rules on the station-network relationship can be found in the FCC archives available to the public. See http://www.fcc.gov/aboutus.html.

4 An insightful history of the early growing pains experienced by ABC can be found in Sterling Quinlan, *Inside ABC: American Broadcasting Company's Rise to Power* (New York: Hastings House, 1979).

5 For a behind-the-scenes look at the Fox phenomenon, see Daniel M. Kimmel, *The Fourth Network: How Fox Broke the Rules and Reinvented Television* (Chicago: Ivan R. Dee Publishing, 2004).

Chapter 9

1 Richard Siklos, "This Time, the Revolution Will Be Televised," *New York Times*, 22 January 2006, Inside the News, p. 5.

2 Adam Thierer, "Why Mass Media Mergers Are Meaningless," *The Free Man: Ideas on Liberty*, January 1995, p. 5. Heritage Foundation Archive. See www.heritage.org/Press/Commentary.

3 Michael Lewis, "The End of the Mass Market," *New York Times Magazine*, 13 April 2000, p. 36.

4 Tom Zeller, "A Generation Serves Notice: It's a Moving Target," *New York Times*, 22 January 2006, Sunday Business Section, p. 1.

5 Glen Dickson, "Broadcasters Cut Out of Convergence," *Broadcasting and Cable*, 16 January 2006, p. 38.

6 Nielsen Media Research and TiVo have a contractual agreement to provide DVR ratings in conjunction with the research company's many other client reports. See www.nielsenmedia.com.

7 Ted Koppel, "And Now a Word for Our Demographic," *New York Times*, 29 January 2006, Op-Ed Section, p. 16.

8   Page Albiniak, "New Ways to Get Rich," *Broadcasting and Cable*, 19 April 2004, p. 1.

9   Steve McClellen, "The Venerable AI Is Mulling New Curley Cues," *Broadcasting and Cable*, 27 October 2003, p. 34.

10 Edward Wasserman, "Internet Companies Concentrating Power," *Miami Herald*, 6 February 2006, p. 23A.

Index

Media Industries

General Editor
David Sumner

The Media Industries series offers comprehensive, classroom friendly textbooks designed to meet the needs of instructors teaching introductory media courses. Each book provides a concise, practical guide to all aspects of a major industry. These volumes are an ideal reference source for anyone contemplating a career in the media.

To order other books in this series, please contact our Customer Service Department:

(800) 770-LANG (within the U.S.)
(212) 647-7706 (outside the U.S.)
(212) 647-7707 FAX

Or order online at www.peterlang.com